THE MAKING

SHREWSE

The Making of
SHREWSBURY
The History of a Border Town

VIVIEN BELLAMY

Wharncliffe
Local History

SHREWSBURY
MUSEUMS
SERVICE

First published in Great Britain in 2004 by
Wharncliffe Local History
an imprint of
Pen & Sword Books Ltd
47 Church Street
Barnsley
South Yorkshire
S70 2AS

ISBN 1-903425-87-5

A CIP catalogue record for this book
is available from the British Library

Typeset (in 10.8/15.8 Plantin Light),
edited and designed by Roger Chesneau
Printed and bound in Singapore by
Kyodo Printing Co. (Singapore) Pte Ltd

Pen & Sword Books Ltd incorporates the imprints of
Pen & Sword Aviation, Pen & Sword Maritime, Pen & Sword Military,
Wharncliffe Local History, Pen and Sword Select, Pen and Sword
Military Classics and Leo Cooper.

For a complete list of Pen & Sword titles please contact
PEN & SWORD BOOKS LIMITED
47 Church Street, Barnsley, South Yorkshire, S70 2AS, England
E-mail: enquiries@pen-and-sword.co.uk
Website: www.pen-and-sword.co.uk

CONTENTS

c. AD 120	Wroxeter a well-established Roman town
410	Roman armies withdraw
c. 450	First Saxons arrive
658	Anglo-Saxon kingdom of Mercia covers Shropshire
757–96	Construction of Offa's Dyke
901	Shrewsbury fortified by Ethelfleda
1066	The Norman Conquest
1071	The Marcher Lordships established:Shrewsbury granted to Roger de Montgomery
1084	Shrewsbury Abbey built
1092	Death of Earl Roger
1102	Rebellion of Robert de Belesme; control of Shrewsbury passes to the Crown
1138	Stephen of Blois seizes Shrewsbury Castle from forces of the Empress Matilda; the Abbey takes possession of the remains of St Winefred
1154	Matilda's son crowned as Henry II; Shrewsbury's first charter
1189	Richard I grants charter
1199	King John allows the town to elect two bailiffs
1215	Magna Carta signed; the Welsh seize Shrewsbury
1240	Town walls completed
1254	Arrival of the Augustinian Friars
1270–72	Guildhall built; The Square paved
1282	The Welsh Prince Llewelyn defeated by Edward I; his brother Dafydd executed in Shrewsbury
1305	Merchant Richard Stury travels to Antwerp to set up trading post
1322	Edward II visits Shrewsbury raising funds to fight Mortimer
1326	Mortimer's rebellion
1346	English victory at the Battle of Crécy
1348–68	The Black Death: sporadic outbreaks kill a third of the population of England
1398	Richard II grants charter
1403	The Battle of Shrewsbury
1426	Parts of Wyle Cop rebuilt following fire
1485	The Battle of Bosworth Field: Henry VII's victory ends the Wars of the Roses
1536–42	Acts of Union bring Wales under English rule
1537	Dissolution of the Monasteries
1538	Thomas Jones becomes first Mayor of Shrewsbury
1546	Abbey buildings pass to William Langley
1578	Work starts on construction of Whitehall
1616	Merchant William Rowley constructs brick mansion
1642	Start of the Civil War
1645	Shrewsbury Castle falls to Parliament
1649	Execution of Charles I: England becomes a republic
1662	Restoration of Charles II

Line

1688	Accession of William and Mary: Shrewsbury's charter restored
1694–1700	Lord Bradford builds a townhouse
1698	Celia Fiennes visits
1704	*The Recruiting Officer* set in Shrewsbury
1706	First turnpike roads opened
1745	Salop Infirmary
1761	Visit of John Wesley
1764	Clive of India is Mayor and MP
1770	Construction of the English Bridge
1774	Dr Samuel Johnson visits
1787	Thomas Telford arrives in Shrewsbury
1790–92	New St Chad's church
1793	Construction of Ditherington Flax Mill
1798	Dr Samuel Butler appointed to reform Shrewsbury School
1809	Birth of Charles Darwin
1815-36	Telford builds Holyhead road
1829	Catholic Emancipation
1837	Queen Victoria's accession
1841	Disraeli elected MP for Shrewsbury
1848–49	Arrival of the railway: construction of station
1851	The Great Exhibition
1859	Publication of Darwin's *The Origin of Species*: 32,000 people attend the Old Shrewsbury Show
1881	Formation of King's Shropshire Light Infantry
1882	Shrewsbury School moves to Kingsland
1900	Opening of Coleham Pumping Station and Shrewsbury's first commercial garage
1918	Death of Wilfred Owen in World War I
1919	Shrewsbury ceases to be main line station
1920	Garden suburb laid out at Ditherington: Castle owned by Shropshire Horticultural Society
1922	Construction of inner ring road
1927	Mary Webb buried in Shrewsbury cemetery
1940	Wartime evacuees in Shrewsbury
1952	Accession of Elizabeth II
1959	Livestock market moves to Harlescott
1968	Telford New Town designated
1974	Local Government reorganisation
1982	Opening of new museum at Rowley's House
1984	Opening of Shropshire Regimental Museum at the Castle
1988–89	Pride Hill and Darwin Shopping centres open
1992	IRA bomb Castle; Shrewsbury bypass and extension of new A5 link to M54 built
2004	New civic offices for Shrewsbury and Atcham District Council open

CKNOWLEDGEMENTS

The compiling of this brief history has depended heavily on the scholarship of others, including that enshrined in the much-treasured *Victoria History of Shropshire* and in Barrie Trinder's excellent *A History of Shropshire*. My warmest personal thanks must go to Tony Carr of Shropshire Archives for unstintingly imparting knowledge and correcting detail, all with immense good humour. In addition, Mike Stokes, Nigel Baker, George Baugh and Tony Crowe have all generously given their time and expert advice, as has my friend and collaborator in this project, Mary White of Shrewsbury Museums.

Vivien Bellamy
June 2004

ILLUSTRATION ACKNOWLEDGEMENTS

Pages 10, 13, 15, 23: Courtesy of Clwyd-Powys Archaeological Trust; 20, 63: Courtesy of Mike Watson; 21, 22, 32, 35, 36: Courtesy of Bracken Books; 25: Courtesy of the Shropshire Archaeological and Historical Society; 27, 66: Courtesy of Nigel Baker; 43, 48, 60, 76, 86, 95, 98 (top), 109, 112, 113, 117, 120, 121, 125, 128, 131, 139: Courtesy of Shropshire Archives; 62: Courtesy of Jenny Wroe; 81: Courtesy of the National Portrait Gallery, London; 87: Courtesy of Shrewsbury Civic Society; 96 (bottom), 97: Courtesy of the Shropshire Regimental Museum; 99: Courtesy of Sabine Hutchinson (www.virtual-shropshire.co.uk); 116: Courtesy of Mike Stokes; 130 (bottom): Courtesy of Baart Harries Newall; 142: Courtesy of Shrewsbury & Atcham Borough Council; 143: Courtesy of Shrewsbury Tourism. Copyright for all other images is held by Shrewsbury Museums Service.

1   ORIGINS

'The town of Shrewsbury standeth on a Rocky Hill of Stone of a sad
redde earth and Severn soe girdeth all the towne that, saving a little
piece, it were an Isle.'
– John Leland (1506–1552), Antiquary to Henry VIII

SHREWSBURY'S topography is remarkable. The town stands on a rising promontory within a pronounced loop, almost creating an island, in the River Severn. By Tudor times, of course, many of the buildings and features noticeable to a modern visitor were already established.

However, very little is actually known of the site of Shrewsbury before the tenth century, although there was certainly some kind of religious centre here by that time. The earliest buildings known to have stood within the loop of the river are the minster churches of St Mary, said to have been founded by the Anglo-Saxon kings of Mercia, and St Chad, an outpost of an early Bishop of Lichfield. Both were monastic establishments, controlling wide swathes of the Shropshire landscape, and they are believed to have been active by about AD 700. Minsters were large churches, some of which elsewhere later became cathedrals, with a staff of priests to serve the local population.

This was part of a pattern, set right across Christian Europe in early medieval times, for settlements to develop around monastic foundations. An important Shropshire example is the eighth-century Abbey of St Milburga at Much Wenlock, fourteen miles south of Shrewsbury. Milburga was of royal blood, the granddaughter of the Mercian king Penda, whose determination and administrative flair she shared. She managed to acquire extensive landholdings in the area for her foundation, which may well have been established as much for reasons of political as ecclesiastical control. The Anglo-

Aerial view of Shrewsbury.

Saxon period saw considerable respect and autonomy accorded to women and, like St Hilda in Northumbria, Milburga ruled a double house of monks and nuns. Her monastery was the dominant religious foundation in Shropshire until the coming of the Normans several hundred years later.

Although such early religious communities were generally sited in remote places, almost inevitably they attracted further settlement. Hence Shrewsbury's site would have become the focus of trade. The

This great inscription, now in Shrewsbury Museum & Art Gallery, was sited on an arch at the entrance to the forum of Roman Wroxeter. A fine example of the letter-cutter's art, it records the visit of the Emperor Hadrian to the city in AD 122.

resulting community would have combined simple timber dwellings with cultivated land and grazing for livestock. During the Anglo-Saxon period it was an ideal spot to offer protection from hostile outsiders, together with land for food production. Nevertheless, much of this is conjecture: there is no archaeological evidence of settlement here before the eighth century, and we know nothing definite about it until two hundred years later. In any case, as a town, Shrewsbury was a relative latecomer in the region (although it pre-dates Ludlow, Oswestry and Bridgnorth, all of which were post-Conquest).

Roman Wroxeter

It was the Romans who founded the first regional capital, at Wroxeter, five miles south-east of the Shrewsbury site. The great empire builders came to this country in AD 43 but they did not consolidate their hold over the midlands until thirty years later, when they established a series of fortresses along the frontier with Wales. By 122 the fort at Wroxeter had become the fourth largest city in Roman Britain, controlling the tribal area

An elaborately decorated silver hand-mirror, found at Wroxeter, demonstrates the sophisticated craftsmanship available in first-century Roman Britain.

Shrewsbury Placenames

Shrewsbury has several unusual and mysterious street names. The steep thoroughfare that enters the town from the English Bridge, up which the coaches used to clatter in the eighteenth century, is Wyle Cop. *Cop* is a fairly widespread ancient name for a hill top (as in Mow Cop in Derbyshire) and *Hwylfa* is Welsh for a steep hill. Mardol is thought to be the name of a devil: perhaps this is a reference to the evil smells that emanated from the tanneries in this insalubrious riverside area! The name of the main shopping street, Pride Hill, refers to the important Pride family who lived here, while Shoplatch (originally Scheteplachlode) is the house of another local clan, the Schuttes. Butcher Row, Milk Street and Fish Street are reminders that traders in a particular commodity were generally found together. The town's red-light district is remembered in Grope (originally the even ruder Gropecount) Lane. The Norman period in Shrewsbury has left us the names Claremont and Murivance, and both these are topographical, deriving from the Latin, *mons* being a hill and *mur* a wall. Frankwell, the area over the Welsh bridge whose inhabitants did not pay taxes to the town, comes from the old French word *franc*, meaning free. The suburb of Harlescott, north of the town, probably remembers the cottage, or homestead, of Heorulaf, a personal name of Scandinavian origin.

of the Cornovii, and known as Viroconium Cornoviorum. It was important enough to be visited by the Emperor Hadrian and continued to develop throughout the lengthy Roman period.

By the fifth century the empire's frontiers were beginning to crumble and Rome was forced to recall its troops to defend itself. When Roman troops withdrew from Britain in AD 410, Wroxeter maintained something of its old role under the control of the Cornovii, now a fully Romanised British tribe. It is often forgotten that native rulers controlled this area during the fifth, sixth and seventh centuries, a period almost as long as that of Roman dominance.

However, the Romans' brilliantly effective administrative machine was gone. Money was no longer minted and hence the circulation of coinage drew to an end; commerce in the old sense seems to have collapsed by 450. The city of Wroxeter was probably finally abandoned during the sixth century because it covered a large area and was impossible to defend without a numerous and well-organised army. It may be that Shrewsbury offered a more easily defensible site for previous inhabitants of Wroxeter.

Alternatively, there is earlier evidence of important settlements, both at the summit of the Wrekin and at Baschurch, north of Shrewsbury. Either of these might have functioned as a regional power base for native rulers before the coming of the Saxons.

Saxon Shropshire

The British kingdom of Powis, which included what is now Shropshire, remained stable for many generations after the departure of the Romans. Nevertheless, the period was one of tribal conflict and, as today, increasing migration throughout Europe. Britain was a target for the Germanic tribes moving westwards but also, in the north and west, for Picts, Scots and Irish.

The Berth, Baschurch. This is thought to have been the site of the death in battle of the British prince, Cynddylan.

The Wrekin

This famous landmark is the site of an Iron Age hill fort which was probably the administrative centre for the area that is now Shropshire. Not in itself a volcano, it is nevertheless composed of Pre-Cambrian volcanic rock that withstood the erosion of softer rock around it. But legend tells another story of its origins.

A malevolent Welsh giant hatched a plan to drown the English town of Shrewsbury, by causing the River Severn to flood. He set off with a large sack of earth with which to build a dam, but, because he was not very bright, he soon got lost. Spying a cobbler pushing a cart full of customers' boots in need of repair, he asked the way. The cobbler, an intelligent man with a good business in the town, was immediately suspicious. 'Well, sir,' he cunningly replied, 'it be a long way for sure. I bin on the road many a weary mile. See here, all these boots are my old ones, worn out on the way!' The giant was cross, and he was also weary of the heavy sack of stones and soil. Disheartened, he turned to go back to Wales and threw the sack down – and that is how the Wrekin came to be where it is!

From early in the fifth century mercenary warriors from Saxony, known for their military prowess, had been invited into Britain by native leaders to defend tribal settlements in regional disputes. The incomers became increasingly numerous and powerful and eventually some turned against their employers, seizing their land. In 446 British chiefs made what must have been a vain appeal to the Roman commander in Gaul for help against the Saxons. In time a series of Saxon kingdoms emerged, the first in Kent: the most powerful, the West Saxon kingdom (Wessex), was founded around 495. However, a hundred years later Shropshire was still under British control, although this was not to last.

Saxon culture was generally based on farmsteads and villages and had no need for urban settlements. However, its power in Britain grew during the sixth century and a capital did spring up, at York, the focus of an area then known as Deira.

A carved bronze disc (shown actual size), found near Cockshutt in north Shropshire. This is the only piece of pagan Saxon metalwork to have been discovered in Shropshire.

Anglo-Saxon settlements in the midlands would have looked to Tamworth, seat of the Mercian dynasty, for political leadership and military protection. The second half of the seventh century in Shropshire is therefore dominated by the figure of Offa, a monarch of European prestige, who dealt on equal terms with the great European Christian ruler, Charlemagne.

In Shropshire the old British ruling families, their influence on the wane, gradually retreated to Wales. In 658 the region and its people, by this time known as the Wroecensaetan, came under the control of the Saxon Wulfhere, a son of the famous Penda. Penda was king of Mercia, a name that refers to the march (or border) with Wales, but he created a more extensive kingdom than this, occupying roughly what is now the West Midlands. During the seventh and eighth centuries, from a power base at Tamworth, Mercian kings controlled all England except East Anglia. Wulfhere, who reigned between 657 and 675, was deeply engaged in tribal conflict; he threw off the domi-

Offa's magnificent earthwork Dyke, constructed between 757 and 796 and running north–south almost from coast to coast for a hundred miles, is now thought to have constituted a boundary rather than a fortification.

nance of Northumbria and invaded Wessex. Like the other sons of Penda, he became a Christian.

It was Wulfhere who established control over the native population, the Wroecansaetan, and during his reign Christianity was adopted by the Mercians. However, there is a notable absence of pagan graves from Shropshire and it is now thought that Christian beliefs and rites dating from the Roman era may well have continued in use among the British tribes. The term 'Dark Ages' to describe the period between the departure of the Romans from these islands and the Norman Conquest is now considered misleading, ignoring as it does the high level of sophisticated culture maintained among the priestly and warrior classes. Nevertheless, more remains to be learned from archaeology about a period in British history, between 350 and 650, lasting almost as long as that of Roman occupation.

In particular, the remains of buildings at Roman Wroxeter now indicate that habitation continued there well into the Saxon period

Ethelfleda, Lady of the Mercians

One of Alfred's achievements had been a treaty with the Danes by which these hitherto unstoppable conquerors agreed not to move beyond their own English territories, which became known as the Danelaw. It was Alfred's determined daughter, Ethelfleda, known as Lady of the Mercians but effectively queen regnant, who launched Shrewsbury's recorded history when she recognised its strategic role on the Welsh border early in the tenth century. The Saxon word *burh* (related to the German word *burg*), indicating a fortified settlement, came into use when, with her brother Ethelred who then ruled Wessex, she created a string of such strongholds in her midlands realm. These were defence posts against the Danes, who by now controlled much of England north of Watling Street. The burh of Shrewsbury, referred to in a charter of Ethelfelda, was linked with other bridge points at Gloucester and Worcester. This status as part of the defensive chain from Chester to Chepstow was not entirely an advantage for Shrewsbury, as political significance led to involvement in military campaigns, with the danger and expense that that entailed. Lady Ethelfleda's tough stance seems to have deterred any Danish military advance into the region, but, nonetheless, by the eleventh century England did have a Danish ruler.

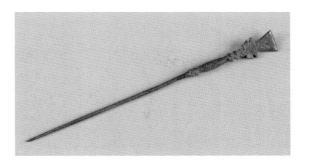

A high level of civilised living is suggested by this tenth-century decorative stylus, used for writing in wax. It was found in 1889 at the Old St Chad's site. Anglo-Saxon pottery has also been found in the town.

and that it was probably the base for local chiefs who maintained Roman traditions as best they could, erecting large timber houses with porticos in a classical style. At least five phases of building have been discovered, leading to the conclusion that the site was occupied until the sixth century. At this time a declining population made the town impossible to defend against the depredations of less civilised tribes. This pattern was reflected in other urban centres, and the focus of life seems to have reverted to smaller rural settlements. The new regional centre of power was probably a hill fort, either on the Wrekin or at the Berth, Baschurch.

Serious attempts were being made to convert the whole of the British Isles to Christianity, and in 597 the Roman Augustine became the first Archbishop of Canterbury. Missionaries from Ireland (where Christianity had flourished from the fifth century) were evangelising in the north. There is no firm evidence of Christian practice in Shrewsbury until the beginning of the tenth century, when we know of the two Anglo-Saxon minsters within the loop of the river.

Offa's reign, alongside that of the Saxon king Alfred the Great (who ruled from 871 to 899 and whose southern kingdom of Wessex later became the dominant region), represents the Golden Age of Anglo-Saxon power. Even before Offa's death, England was threatened in 793 by sea-borne invaders from Scandinavia. Initially at least, these ferocious pagan warriors with their great ships brought destruction and terror to settlements and unarmed religious houses. Offa's Christian kingdom succumbed to Danish power in 874, and it is revealing that his successor, Burgred, chose to make the great Christian centre of Rome his place of refuge. The Danes, or Vikings, established a base at Jorvik (York), and excavations there have shown them to have been craftsmen, traders and farmers as well as warriors. The tide of their influence in the midlands ebbed at the end of the ninth century, largely as a result of the efforts of Alfred the Great and his children.

The first reference we have to Shrewsbury, giving us its early English name Scrobbesbyrig, occurs in a royal document which was witnessed here in AD 901. Scrobbesbyrig roughly translates as 'the fortified place in the scrubland'. The town became the focus of a new administrative entity, the shire, early in the tenth century. It is likely that these new land units were created as a means of controlling the region more efficiently in the face of the Scandinavian military threat. The Mercian shires were based on units of taxation called hides, and the 2,400 hides of Shropshire included, as well as the land of the Wroecensaetan, a substantial slice of the neighbouring Magonsaetan tribe's territory.

By about AD 900 St Mary's and St Chad's churches probably continued to represent foundations for, respectively, the king and the bishop. The market place was sited centrally, between the churches of St Mary and St Alkmund, the latter, according to tradition, established in the tenth century by the Lady Ethelfleda. The market's main business was in wool and leather goods, as in later times. It was quite probably here that livestock were slaughtered, and along nearby Butcher Row local people would buy the freshly killed meat that was so important to their diet. Running with blood and steaming with animal offal and dung, this area would have been no place for squeamish modern sensibilities.

By now the town, like the other midland burhs of Stafford and Warwick, was set up as the focus of the county of Shropshire, providing an administrative base for the king's representative, the shire reeve or sheriff. This official's duties were formalised during the eleventh century. In 937 Alfred the Great's grandson Athelstan defeated an alliance of Scots and Danes at the Battle of Brunanburh. He thus became overlord of the old British territories of Scotland, Wales and Cornwall and gained control of Viking York. We know that Shrewsbury was fortified then because this was a prerequisite for the minting of coins. In the year 1006 there is a documentary reference to Shropshire in the *Anglo-Saxon Chronicle* recording that King Ethelred the Unready had 'gone across the Thames, into Shropshire and received there his food rents in the Christmas season'.

Before 1066 the immediate surroundings of the town were evidently considered well-established and secure enough for a Saxon thane, Siward, a kinsman of Edward the Confessor, to build a hall outside the obvious safety of the river loop. An interesting figure in the early life of Shrewsbury, he established a wooden chapel close by, on the site of the later Abbey. Much of this property would be appropriated, at the Conquest, by the invaders.

Shrewsbury was important and prosperous enough to have its own mint in the late Saxon period, and these are examples of coins surviving from the reign of Athelstan, who is remembered as a wise lawgiver as well as a warrior. Minting coinage was always a movable operation, depending on a 'moneyer' and his equipment, and, contrary to popular belief, did not require fixed premises. Production ceased at the end of Henry III's reign, in 1272, although the minting of coinage in Shrewsbury was revived by Charles I during the Civil War.

2 THE NORMAN CONQUEST

T HE NORMANS, a name derived from the people's origins as Norse or Scandinavian settlers, were the toughest and most successful racial group in eleventh-century Europe. They were also skilful seafarers across the Mediterranean and created a kingdom in Sicily. William, Duke of Normandy, was nominally the vassal of the king of France, but nobody would have dared to argue with him.

The Conqueror's invasion of Britain, in the summer of 1066, heralded what was probably the most rapid and comprehensive alteration to life these islands had seen – in spite of the fact that the life of the Royal Court was already heavily influenced by Norman ways. King Edward the Confessor, thus known because of the depth of his religious devotion (which led to a refusal to consummate his marriage and hence probably to the Conquest itself), was a member of the Saxon royal dynasty of Wessex. However, he had spent the twenty-eight years of Danish rule over England in Normandy, and

The Normans brought with them craftsmen who introduced Romanesque styles of building and decoration. This carving on the porch of St Mary's dates from about 1100.

Detail of Bayeux tapestry.

when he became king he brought with him a host of Norman advisers. Naturally there were several contenders for the role of his heir. It was said that he had promised the English crown to William of Normandy, but at his death he named as his successor the English earl Harold Godwineson. William, indeed, had solid grounds for his assertion that Edward the Confessor had intended the crown for him – among other things, his wife was directly descended from Alfred the Great – but it was Harold who became king, and soon after his coronation, in a battle near York, he defeated Harold Hardrada of Norway, who was also after the crown.

The Norman Duke William, however, was a more formidable opponent. King Harold had to take him on immediately following the victory over the Norwegians and an arduous march south for his exhausted soldiers. At Hastings, as is well known, Harold was killed, and William's progress to the English crown was now irresistible. England at this time was a highly successful agrarian economy, and, although William returned to his Norman duchy, it remained the jewel in his crown.

Perhaps because far more historical documents than ever before survive for this period, all over Europe, our knowledge of the changes brought by the Conquest is substantial. For a start, the Normans made French, rather than English, the everyday language of the Court (administration and business were recorded in Latin), and England became deeply connected to a web of European affairs. Henceforward until the thirteenth century the king of England would have plenty of French blood in his veins.

Social and contractual arrangements in feudal times depended on the idea that all land was held by permission of the monarch. He was thus able to reward his nobles through gifts of land, in return for which they were obliged to provide him with military support. Thus William the Conqueror automatically took control of the entire territory without regard to existing landholdings.

Earl Roger

In 1071, two years after crushing a major rebellion against him in the north of England, King William I granted his kinsman Roger de Montgomery a large swathe of land through the midlands and Welsh march. The territory centred on the county of Shropshire, and Roger was also granted the Saxon title of Earl. For the next thirty years Earl Roger's family maintained more or less autonomous power in the region. This was a result of the king's decision to base his administration of the difficult Welsh march on this and two other new earldoms – Chester and Hereford. These three Marcher earls became immensely powerful, supported in Shropshire by a group of lower-ranking noble families like the Fitzalans, Fitzwarines and Corbets. Keeping the Welsh

The Fitzwarines

This Anglo-Norman family is celebrated in a thirteenth-century prose romance. They were minor marcher lords who erected Whittington Castle and struggled for dominance over rival families in this lawless border area. These frequently bloody feuds continued for several generations, although the story employs considerable poetic licence in attributing all the heroic deeds to one central character, Fulke Fitzwarine (whose coat of arms is shown left). The family lived at Whittington until 1420.

Whittington Castle from the air.

under control was the king's main aim, but the power of these war-lords was not always to the king's advantage.

Roger of Montgomery, Earl of Shrewsbury, used the town as a base for his raids into Wales and the town was therefore an important source of men and provisions, and hence of trade, with the surrounding area. Roger's task was to keep the local populace under control, and for this reason his priority was to construct a large timber castle. Limewashed a dazzling white, as was usual for Norman strongholds as protection against fire, decay and vermin, it must have had a huge visual and psychological impact on the cowed local population. As elsewhere, the construction of the castle was carried out with considerable ruthlessness towards the local people, and over fifty more humble dwellings were razed to the ground to make room for it. We know nothing of the many people who were so arbitrarily rendered homeless.

Noblemen such as Earl Roger belonged to a self-perpetuating warrior-caste at the top of the social scale. In order to retain this preeminence, they had to demonstrate strength and aggression as well as intelligence. Literacy was quite unnecessary, administrative and legal matters being dealt with by educated scribes and officials who were monks. The king had to be on his mettle to maintain his own position amongst his peers. Like other powerful barons in this particular tough group, Roger was not always reliable in his loyalty, in spite of the many benefits he had received from the king.

The Welsh were a racial group closer than any other to the native Britons and were never fully subdued by the Normans. Almost immediately after campaigning against them, in 1088, the earl led an unsuccessful rebellion against his old comrade's son, King William Rufus. However, an uneasy peace was finally made before Roger died in 1094.

Saxon Rebels and Remnants

Whilst the new Norman administrative apparatus was immensely successful in its domination of the native population, it is now known that a number of Saxon noblemen did succeed in accommodating themselves comfortably enough to the new regime. The thane Siward, mentioned earlier, demonstrates that the obliteration of Saxon interests may not have been as complete as has been thought. He had not

Edric the Wild

By 1069, while William was campaigning in the north of England, the Norman garrison housed in the castle at Shrewsbury was attacked and besieged by the Anglo-Saxon nobleman Edric. It was a serious rebellion against the occupying forces, supported by warriors from Cheshire and Wales and 'other untameable Englishmen'. They set fire to the town before retreating beyond their adversaries' reach.

Edric the Wild, as he was known, acquired a legendary reputation. It was said that he married a fairy princess and that those walking late on a moonlit night along Wenlock Edge may glimpse the apparition of this couple wildly galloping their horses! Edric's resistance, though, was real enough and may have prompted the establishment of more formidable defences for the town.

Reconstruction of Roger de Montgomery's motte-and-bailey castle at Hen Domen, near Welshpool. Built to protect part of Earl Roger's military fiefdom in Shropshire and the Welsh March, Shrewsbury's castle would have had much the same appearance. Unlike other fortresses in this part of Shropshire, it was the earl's personal preserve.

fought against the Norman invasion at Hastings and evidently possessed some diplomatic skill. He contrived to make a deal with the new king whereby his Shrewsbury property, including the hall that he had built for himself, passed to the crown but he retained his other estates. The wooden chapel that he had built was replaced in 1084 by the far grander and more permanent stone structure of Shrewsbury Abbey. Not all Saxon leaders were prepared to make such accommodations, and there was some fierce localised resistance.

The Castle
The conquerors marked their presence on these shores by constructing a range of imposing new building types, in particular the castle.

Hitherto, fortifications had surrounded settlements or farms and had sought to offer protection for a whole community. These huge piles were quite different. Their purpose, as the quotation in the accompanying caption suggests, was to shelter an alien élite, and to overawe the local population.

The earliest defensive systems were usually established for the purpose of protecting an entire community against raiders from elsewhere. The concept of the castle, constructed to secure the position of the ruling class, was exploited with brilliant efficiency by the invading warlords from Normandy. At this period the castle's purpose was not so much to defend the town as to intimidate potential troublemakers.

Nothing remains of the fabric of Earl Roger's timber castle. However, a geophysical survey commissioned by Shrewsbury Museums in 2001 demonstrates that it was a mighty structure indeed. The remaining earth ramparts are original and the motte (mound) was much larger than the existing high ground within the castle precinct suggests. Part of the steep slope fell away when the river altered course in the 1270s. The Great Tower, built on the motte to provide a final bolt-hole for all the castle's inhabitants, was forty feet square and stood at least fifty feet high. Until the final collapse, it would have co-existed with the stone buildings below. The Great Hall which today houses the Shropshire regimental collections is substantially a royal construction of the mid-thirteenth century and would have provided living and eating space for king and court. The bailey, or walled yard of the castle, provided accommodation for servants, livestock, horses and equipment. The inner bailey, or courtyard, offered accommodation for the knights of the county during their forty days' annual military service for the king,

Earl Roger was immensely powerful, and even the youngest of his sons was given control of an area as large as the whole of south Lancashire. Nonetheless, life was precarious and Roger's line in this

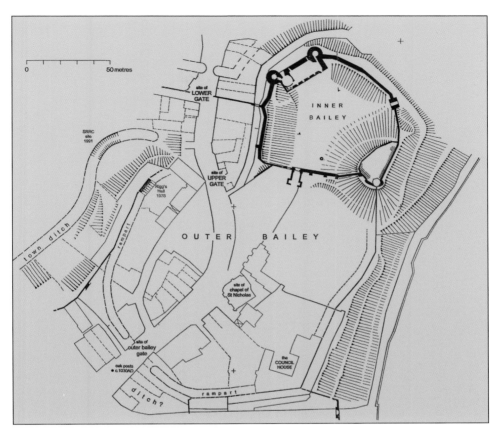

Map of medieval castle layout showing inner and outer baileys According to the chronicler William de Poitiers, it was built 'against the fickleness of the vast and fierce population'.

country died out fairly swiftly when his only surviving son, Robert de Belesme, disgraced himself. Medieval kings depended on the support of military henchmen, but this could sometimes backfire and did so in the case of Robert. He had masterminded yet another rebellion against the Conqueror's son, Henry I, during which he fortified Bridgnorth in 1102, but he was defeated and sent packing back to Normandy. The town of Shrewsbury then reverted to the direct ownership of the king. He made a gift of it to his second wife, Adela, who chose as her deputy William FitzAlan. From this moment the FitzAlan family played a major role in medieval Shropshire and were later famed for, among other things, their production in the county of that very valuable medieval commodity the warhorse.

Henry I made serious efforts to reconcile the English (as they were now called) with the Normans and married a Scottish princess of Anglo-Saxon descent. His tragedy was the loss of both his sons when their ship sank in the English Channel. He became determined that his sole remaining child, his daughter Matilda, should succeed him as monarch. This had disastrous consequences following his death, for the peace of the country and the wellbeing of Shrewsbury.

3 A MEDIEVAL FORTRESS-TOWN

AS A CLIENT of the royal house, the Sheriff of Shrewsbury, William FitzAlan, supported the claims of Henry I's daughter Matilda to the English throne. When this lady married Geoffrey Count of Anjou, she rather surprisingly managed to retain the title of Empress from her first marriage to the Holy Roman Emperor. Her father had made his barons swear to accept her accession but they were not happy to accept the rule of a woman, even the granddaughter of William the Conqueror, whose arrogance and determination she inherited. Although declared Lady of the English, she was never crowned queen. The barons were divided and many supported the claims of her cousin, Stephen, Count of Blois, the son of William I's daughter. A bitter war between the factions ensued. In 1138 Stephen besieged and took Shrewsbury Castle amid considerable slaughter. For eighteen terrible years, a period which became known as The Anarchy, the whole of England was ravaged by this civil war. Eventually Matilda retired to her husband's French territo-

The stone castle.

Eleanor of Aquitaine

Eleanor was a royal heiress and a woman gifted with determination and intelligence as well as the ability to captivate men. Such was her reputation that it was said that the great Islamic leader Saladin had been her lover – although in truth this is most improbable. She was divorced by the French king because she did not produce an heir, but as the Queen of England she had four sons, including Richard I and King John. However, her marriage to Henry, who was eleven years younger, did not last and she encouraged her sons to rebel against him. She lived to what was then the great age of eighty-two and died in Normandy.

---

ries in Anjou, and these gave their name to the Angevin dynasty she founded.

In 1154 Matilda's son was crowned Henry II, the first king since the Conquest to inherit without opposition. Through his queen, Eleanor, the former wife of Louis VII of France and the daughter of the Duke of Aquitaine, he acquired still vaster areas of that country. In 1158 he visited Shrewsbury and, perhaps in recognition of its loyalty to his mother, halved its level of taxation. Shrewsbury was ruled directly by the King almost until the end of the twelfth century.

Today, two massive red sandstone drum towers and a flanking wall dominate the narrow strip of land which forms the approach to Shrewsbury from the north. This stone building, and indeed most of the Castle's structure, dates from the reign of Henry III (1216–1272) and consisted of a great hall with an undercroft or basement for storage, with private accommodation in the two towers.

Conflict with Wales

While King William's war machine, with its extensive castle-building programme, had succeeded in subduing the English population fairly rapidly, Wales, with its mountainous terrain, was a harder nut to crack. Norman barons made good headway into the southern lowlands and intermarried with Welsh princely families. Llewelyn the Great (1173–1240) was himself married to a natural daughter of the English King

John, although this did little to prevent major conflict between 1211 and 1234. The northern mountain ranges favoured Welsh guerrilla tactics, and the marches of Wales, from Chester southwards, were a battleground for many generations.

During Henry III's reign Shrewsbury Castle housed a garrison on constant alert for trouble from Wales. That mountainous region had become more confident and united under Llewelyn's leadership. The shifting nature of this long-drawn-out conflict is illustrated by the fact that Shrewsbury was briefly taken by the Welsh in 1215, the year before Henry acceded to the throne. Llewelyn was able to sweep in and sack the town, and twenty years later Welsh raiders set fire to the suburb of Frankwell.

During the later Norman period several royal grants were made to the town for the construction and repair of walls, work which was largely complete by 1240. The earliest evidence of the walls around Shrewsbury, running from the top of the slope near the Castle along the line of the modern road by the Raven Meadows car park, dates from this period.

Henry III was an able monarch but his reign was dogged by difficulties, not least the Barons' Rebellion of 1264, led by

Tower on town walls.

The Fitz Alans

John le Fitz Alain

In efforts to contain the troublesome Welsh, the King was forced to grant increasing privileges to the marcher lordships and this inevitably began to erode royal power. The FitzAlan family began their rise to prominence in the service of Henry I, the Conqueror's son, who ascended the throne in 1100, and his queen, Adela. Fourteen years after this they are recorded as controlling the lordship of Oswestry. In 1155 William FitzAlan married the heiress of Clun, Isabel de Say, and by the second half of the twelfth century the family was established as a force to be reckoned with, both in Shropshire and in Welsh areas where they collected rents and taxes. They had immense power locally, operating courts and controlling the movement of people living within their jurisdiction. In 1138 the resourceful William managed to escape the siege of Shrewsbury and later returned triumphantly.

There was rivalry between the FitzAlans and the other marcher lords, the Corbets of Caus and the Mortimers; angry confusion often arose when those accused of crime could escape into the territory of a rival and claim sanctuary!

The coat-of-arms of the FitzAlans is shown above left. From the middle of the fourteenth century the family's interests became largely concentrated in their estates in the south of England. The present Duke of Norfolk, of Arundel Castle in Sussex, is the current representative.

Simon de Montfort, Earl of Leicester. Hence this period was one of vigorous castle building and repair. These activities brought money and work to the townspeople of Shrewsbury. During the 1260s, for example, it is known that a local engineer was contracted to provide bolts for a giant crossbow and to repair the town's siege engine. Gates, walls and bridges were all improved by order of the Sheriff and Keeper of the Castle. The Castle's peripheral location made the town, in effect, an extended bailey within its own walls.

Llewelyn the Last (c. 1228–1282) maintained a close alliance with his illustrious father-in-law, Simon de Montfort, leader of the baronial resistance to the throne which led in 1215 to the Magna Carta. Simon's great achievement was to bring about the earliest parliaments, forcing the King to negotiate with his barons and thereby limiting the hitherto absolute power of the monarch. Simon died in 1265 at the Battle of Evesham, the last great civil conflict before the Battle of Shrewsbury in 1403. Prince Llewelyn himself won a series of victories and was the first actually to call himself Prince of Wales. He was killed in battle near Builth Wells in 1282. His brother Dafydd was executed in Shrewsbury later that year by the horrifyingly brutal method of hanging, drawing and quartering. It is said that the decision to carry out this execution was made at the Parliament held that year in the great barn at Acton Burnell (the gable ends of which can still be seen). At that period parliaments were held in different parts of the country – wherever the King happened to be – and this one was unusual, although not unique, in that it included commoners as well as the great nobility.

The deaths of the two Welsh princes marked the end of King Edward I's campaigns in Wales. By the close of the thirteenth century large-scale resistance had been crushed, although it continued to reappear fitfully.

Dynastic Wars

A serious fire tore through Shrewsbury during the 1390s, and by the end of the decade, at the accession of Henry IV, the Castle was described as 'ruinous', a term which indicated merely that it had fallen into disrepair for military purposes. Its Great Tower, the symbol of aggressive military

A fanciful portrait of Owain Glyndŵr, from a local public house sign. In Shakespeare's Henry IV *the Welsh leader is characterised as a Celtic magician.*

domination, had collapsed a century earlier and not been replaced. Although it was still the property of the King, its repair was clearly no longer economically viable. As a result of this, and of the related fact that Montgomery Castle had taken over some of its functions, Shrewsbury lost its role as a 'front-line' base. However, it was destined once more to figure dramatically in history.

The charismatic Welsh leader Owain Glyndŵr was born around 1354, and as a result of personal grievances against Henry IV of England he had managed by 1400 to seize control of most of Wales. Declaring himself Prince of Wales, he held parliaments and made treaties with other countries. Allying himself with the disgruntled Percy family of Northumberland, he was involved in the rebellion that led to the famous Battle of Shrewsbury, which took place on 21 July 1403.

The Welsh border, with its powerful marcher families, continued to be a source of irritation to the Crown. Shrewsbury was a power base for Richard II and in1398 he arranged for parliament to sit at the

Richard II, from the Charter he issued in 1398.

Jousting knights.

Abbey. Determined to consolidate his power, the King had his officials assemble all the men of fighting age and ability in Shrewsbury. They then confiscated all the armour and weapons which the town

The Council of the March

Like many border areas, the Welsh march was chronically plagued with casual violence, cattle rustling and murder. This was gradually brought under royal control. In 1471 Edward IV set up a Council to look after the affairs of his infant son, the Prince of Wales, and four years later its remit was extended to cover the counties of Worcestershire, Gloucestershire, Herefordshire and Shropshire. By these means, and the practice of settling the royal heir at Ludlow Castle in the care of a President of the Council, the lawlessness of the border area was brought to an end. Shropshire provided more members of the Council than any other county and Shrewsbury was an important base. Queen Elizabeth's President of the Council was Sir Henry Sidney, father of the poet Philip (who was at school here). Elaborate festivities surrounded his visit in 1581, and his departure, by river barge, was graced with madrigals performed by pupils of the school, all dressed in green and with willows on their heads!

The marcher lordships disintegrated in 1536 when Wales and England were united, but, although it had outlived its purpose, the Council was not finally dissolved until 1689.

Over My Dead Body!

One of Shrewsbury's responsibilities was to provide fighting men for the Wars of the Roses, and the town's Bailiff, Thomas Mytton, had sworn undying loyalty to Richard III, declaring that the King's Welsh rival would never cross the bridge into the town unless it was 'over his body'. This oath was more than compromised in 1485 at the entry into Shrewsbury of Henry Tudor with a *volte-face* by Mytton, who lay down and allowed Henry to step over his prone body!

---

had provided for its own defence. In spite of these moves, by the following year Richard had lost the crown to Henry Bolingbroke, Duke of Hereford, who was supported by soldiers from Shrewsbury.

The place of Shrewsbury in medieval national life may be gauged from the fact that more than one event is set here in the plays of Shakespeare. One such scene during the Wars of the Roses (the Red Rose of the House of Lancaster versus the White Rose of the Yorkist supporters) dramatises a visit to the town by Richard II. He is shown intervening at the last minute to prevent single combat between the warring dukes of Norfolk and Hereford. The latter was punished by

---

John Talbot, Earl of Shrewsbury

Talbot was a leading knightly figure in the dynastic conflict known as the Wars of the Roses. Born in Whitchurch, he devoted his long life to military service on behalf of Henry VI, for whom he also fought the French. He was almost eighty when he died in 1453, hacked to death by a French battleaxe at Castillon. His soldier son remained at his side and suffered the same fate. The great earl's prowess as a warrior earned him the title 'The English Achilles' and he was recreated as an epic hero more than a hundred years later by Shakespeare:

> *...is this the scourge of France?*
> *Is this the Talbot so much feared abroad*
> *That with his name the mothers still their babes?*

In later years the Talbot family had very little to do with the town. The coat-of-arms of the Talbot family is shown at right.

exile but returned later to become Henry IV. Later he was himself challenged by the coalition that included Owain Glyndŵr.

Events surrounding the Battle of Shrewsbury in 1403 appear in *Henry IV, Part 1*. Four years before the battle, Henry IV had taken the crown from Richard I with the help of the powerful Percy family. The Percys, with their power base in Northumberland, had held the Scottish border for the King but were dissatisfied with the royal display of gratitude. From their estates they were able to persuade large numbers of the late Richard II's former supporters to join a rebel army. Henry Percy, known as Hotspur and a figure of considerable glamour and military experience, rallied two hundred Cheshire knights to the cause. (It is intriguing that Hotspur, although he was forty at

Battlefield Church was built as a chantry, where priests would say masses for the souls of those killed in the ferocious fighting which took place on the afternoon of 21 July, 1403. Estimates of the number slaughtered on that day vary between 6,000 and 20,000. This is a huge number for any episode of a civil war and it has been ascribed to the widespread use of the longbow. This formidable weapon, developed as a hunting weapon during the thirteenth century, was first used en masse *at this battle, and was soon, in 1415, to be so brilliantly successful against the French at Agincourt*

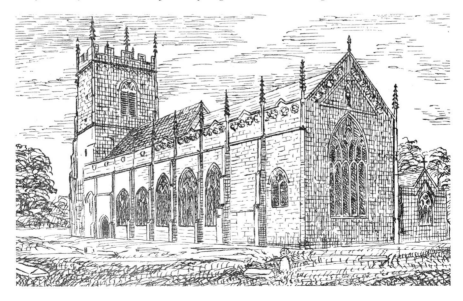

Henry Tudor (later Henry VII) is said to have stayed at this house on his journey from his base in Pembrokeshire. The following day he led his troops through Shrewsbury and on to victory at Bosworth Field, Leicestershire, in 1485. This epic battle is celebrated by Shakespeare, in support of the Tudor dynasty, in the play Richard III.

the time, was always referred to as 'young', and it is a reminder that, although many people did not reach adulthood, those who did might enjoy long lives.) The Battle of Shrewsbury brought victory to Henry IV, but nonetheless his old enemy Glyndŵr was still plaguing the town with raids in 1409.

Well into the fifteenth century England continued to be ravaged by the protracted civil wars between the powerful dynasties of Lancaster and York. In 1459 Shrewsbury was obliged to defend itself again, as a stronghold

This statue, for many years believed to represent the Duke of York, was first erected on the Welsh Bridge when the defences were strengthened in 1458. Its presence indicated the town's support for the Yorkist cause. Fortunately for Shrewsbury, although the Duke was killed shortly afterwards, his son, who had been staying in Shrewsbury, became King Edward IV. The statue was transferred to the Market Hall in The Square only when the bridge was replaced, in 1770. The figure is now believed to be more probably the Black Prince (1330–1376), the son of Edward III.

Ludlow Castle, by Joseph Powell.

of the Yorkist cause. This conflict was not resolved until 1485, when a Welshman, Henry Tudor, took the crown from Richard III at the Battle of Bosworth Field. Marrying Margaret of York, he finally united the Red and White Roses to found the great dynasty of the Tudors.

By the time of Henry VII there was no need for a military presence in Shrewsbury. He began to deprive the hitherto dangerously independent marcher lords of some of their vast territories, and the Acts of Union of 1536 and 1542 brought the whole region under the control of English law. Peace in the march brought more security and prosperity to Shrewsbury, and the Castle was allowed to fall into disrepair. Without a real function to perform, it appears to have been occupied as tenements for local people. However, the building evidently retained some prestige: the record of a tenant's complaint that boys' games had worn the grass bare within the grounds suggests that there was reason to expect that some notice would be taken by the authorities. However this may be, in 1586 Queen Elizabeth granted the structure to the town. In the same year George Talbot, the Earl of Shrewsbury and the realm's premier earl, became Shropshire's first lord lieutenant. This post made him responsible for the mustering of military forces in the county, and it is quite probable that some basic repairs to the Castle were then undertaken.

THE TOWN: TRADING AND MANAGING

'Built on a hill fair Salop greets the eye
While Severn forms a crescent gliding by;
Two bridges cross the navigable stream
And British Alders give the town a name.'
– John Leland

BEFORE the Norman Conquest Shropshire remained relatively undeveloped: only two towns are recorded in the Domesday Book in 1086, Quatford and Shrewsbury. During the century after 1150 there was a proliferation of urban communities and most English towns acquired their legal identity and independence during this period. Medieval monarchs used the granting of charters as a means of fund-raising. Henry I, King of England and Duke of Normandy from 1106, was the first to grant Shrewsbury a charter (which, sadly, does not survive) and in 1189 Richard I granted one that still survives in the town's museum. This allowed the burgesses of Shrewsbury to control the town, in return for forty marks of silver per annum, 'ten marks on account of the two chargers which they used to provide.' Shrewsbury is named Salopsberia in the Charter.

During the thirteenth century the town's Corporation was beginning to provide amenities such as the substantial stone bridges so important for trade and communication, and paving for the main

The town seal, dating from 1425, depicting the four aspects of the town which would have been most important – the red sandstone surrounding walls, the bridges, the river and the churches. The town's defensive walls, completed in the 1270s, fulfilled an economic as well as a defensive function, controlling entry by tolls exacted at the gates. These tolls were collected by leading citizens according to a rota and were an important source of revenue for the town as it was expanding, attracting new settlers with the promise of security and employment.

thoroughfares. The Square was laid out and paved in 1272–75 as a new market place.

From the twelfth century Shrewsbury established commercial links as far afield as York, Hull, London and the ports of the south coast. These connections, combined with its role as a centre for the wool trade, brought considerable prosperity to the town during the Middle Ages. This fact reflects the most marked characteristic of the English economy in the twelfth and thirteenth centuries – economic growth, creating surpluses that could be transformed into building urban communities. Shrewsbury did particularly well and by the early part of the fourteenth century was among the ten wealthiest provincial towns in England.

Guilds, the Corporation and Politics

An essential part of medieval civic, commercial and social life throughout Europe was the organisation of guilds (sometimes called 'crafts'), or companies, of tradesmen and merchants. These guilds controlled the quality and price of work produced by the members, and negoti-

---

Burgage Plots

The feudal system was predicated on ownership and tenancies of land. Subordinates generally gave military service or work on their superior's land in return for the use of plots of their own. Work other than farming, such as blacksmithing, carpentry and textile production, was catered for by a system which excluded military and agricultural obligations. This offered a form of tenancy specific to towns (boroughs) known as burgage holdings. Every plot allowed for a narrow slot on the street for the all-important shop front. Living accommodation was provided on several floors above the shop for the burgess's family, servants and apprentices. The strip of land behind accommodated workshops, storage and room for vegetable-growing, a few chickens, a pig and perhaps a horse and cart. Burgesses formed an urban class neither peasant nor aristocrat which became the basis for the development of the bourgeoisie, or middle class. Their annual rents would be paid to the overlord of the borough, who might be the King or a local lord or bishop. Like other developing market towns, Shrewsbury was laid out in 'burgage' plots, and these layouts survived for several centuries.

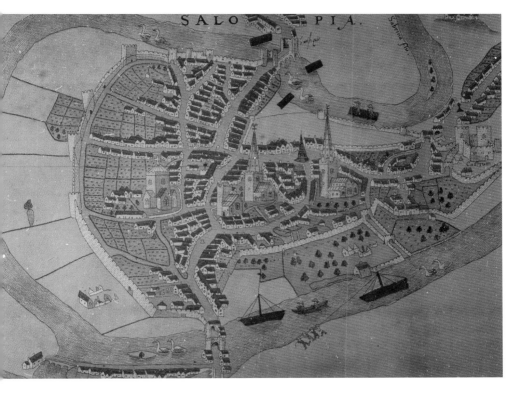

This map, drawn by Burleigh in about 1575, shows a still largely medieval town protected by walls and the gate of the old Welsh Bridge.

ated for their members' benefit. Without licence from the Merchant Guild it was impossible to trade in Shrewsbury, and hence most of the tasks of local government devolved upon this body. The Guild Hall, built in 1270, functioned as the town treasury with a responsibility to ensure fair trading practices. It was administered by the Town Clerk, an important official who had to be able to read and write Latin, the language of officialdom.

Recruitment to the guilds operated through a system of apprenticeship. Boys would be apprenticed to a trade for seven years, becoming journeymen or fully qualified craftsmen after that, free to find work anywhere. It was possible for those with business acumen as well as technical skill to accumulate great personal wealth, although in Shrewsbury, as in other towns, certain merchant families managed to retain economic and political power for many generations.

In towns it was the trade guilds which, as organisations already established, became the basis for local government. Most medieval monarchs found a convenient way to raise money through granting charters to towns, offering them a measure of financial independence and self-government. Hitherto the King had controlled Shrewsbury directly through his officer, the sheriff (shire reeve) of the county. The main duty of this official had originally been to command the shire levy when military reinforcements were required by the King, but inevitably certain judicial functions accrued to the post. Gradually, over time, the townsmen, mainly merchants, took over as they bought rights and privileges from the King. These were confirmed by a series of charters.

In 1199 King John allowed Shrewsbury to elect two officers, called bailiffs, to run the everyday affairs of the town and preside over its courts. Shrewsbury thus became self-governing, using a system based on the bailiffs, a council of twelve thanesmen and other officials. The word 'thane' is of Saxon origin, suggesting an ancient lineage for this feature of local government. Only burgesses whose property and income reached a certain value were entitled to vote, and their families tended to create a self-perpetuating oligarchy. Occasionally there were quarrels amongst the members of this ruling élite. In the 1380s disputes had to be solved by calling in as arbitrators two important local grandees, the Earl of Arundel, the most powerful Shropshire landowner, and the Abbot, whose prestige was comparable. In 1444 the Corporation, as this body became known, was greatly enlarged with Parliamentary approval, but the qualifications remained too narrow for the entry of significant new blood.

By the fifteenth century the two most important crafts in Shrewsbury were those involved with the textile trade – the mercers, who included

Castle Street, by the Rev. E. Pryce Owen. This Victorian artist shows a lively street scene with seventeenth-century timber-framed dwellings now, sadly, demolished.

some metalworkers, and the drapers, dealing in cloth. Both these bodies also fulfilled welfare and charitable functions, providing accommodation in almshouses for their sick and elderly members.

Pavage, Murage and Pontage

The bailiffs were employed by the town's Corporation and were empowered to levy taxes. These paid for street paving, continual repairs to the town's defences, and construction of quays and bridges (referred to in documents as 'pavage, murage and pontage'). Later these duties extended to the mercantile centre, the Guild Hall, as well as to contributions to churches and charitable institutions. Another obligation of the Corporation was to delegate two men to take part in the 'parlements' [*sic*] convened by the King. (These offered opportunities for the King to hear the views of his subjects but, in spite of the name, they were far from democratic bodies in the modern sense.) The king continued to need money and military support and the Corporation was expected to fulfil these requirements unquestioningly. By 1279 the town was paying £30 to the King for various civic privileges, including the important right to charge rent for land. Official payments are recorded in 1322 to armourers, clerks and builders of artillery in respect of preparations to assist Edward II (who had already borrowed £400 personally from three loyal burgesses) against his queen and her lover, the marcher earl Mortimer.

In 1377 the returns of the poll tax allow us to estimate Shrewsbury's population as being about three thousand. As the population expanded and its economic power grew, it offered a challenge to the interests of the Church, which right up to the Dissolution of the Monasteries in the 1530s played a leading part in agriculture, commerce and industry. Many religious orders owned property within the town and operated businesses. At the Abbey's foundation it had been given a large piece of land outside the walls of the town, and this had become a thriving settlement with its own bailiffs and market. The allegiance of this district, known as Abbey Foregate, was naturally to its landlord, the Abbot, and it was quite independent of the town authorities. Hence there were inevitable wrangles between the two communities over trading rights; both bodies, for example, had the right to hold markets and levy taxes on them. Dis-

Fourteenth-century aquamanile, or vessel for use in washing the hands at meals, found in Shrewsbury. Before the advent of the fork, food was eaten using only a knife and hence, among the higher social orders at least, there was a need to remove grease elegantly from the fingers.

Sir John de Charlton and Lady Hawise

One of the reasons for Richard Stury's success was his connection with the influential Sir John de Charlton. Sir John was a somewhat unscrupulous member of the coterie of 'new men' with whom Edward II surrounded himself, to the anger of the hereditary peers. By marrying the powerful Welsh heiress Hawise de Powis, he became master of a large part of the Welsh march and gained the title of Lord Charlton of Powis. In the conflict between Edward II and Queen Isabella and her lover, the Earl of Mortimer, Charlton changed sides more than once, and he was responsible for the brutal execution of the Earl of Arundel. The Charltons' imposing mansion stood at the junction of Shoplatch and St John's Hill.

Sir John de Charlton (1332–1353), as depicted in the Jesse window of St Mary's church.

putes also arose between the town and other religious foundations, such as Haughmond Abbey. It was the responsibility of the two bailiffs to deal as diplomatically as they could with all such conflicts. The Corporation was expected to maintain law and order and to ensure that trading practices were fair.

International Business

Because of Shrewsbury's position on the edge of major sheep-farming areas, wool was the most important business for the town during the Middle Ages. In fact the county of Shropshire dominated the export trade of the entire country. Most of the processes by which wool was made marketable, including cloth-making, were carried out on farms and in small workshops in the countryside, but it was the merchants in the towns who gained the wealth. In 1273 five thousand sacks of wool were exported from England, and 600 of these came from Shropshire merchants. Most of Shrewsbury's leading families, such as the Prides of Pride Hill, were involved with the wool trade.

Charlton Hall, no longer extant, stood at the junction of Shoplatch and St John's Hill. Sir John de Charlton was not the only Shrewsbury magnate to build himself a substantial stone house in the town, but his was probably the most impressive, and it provided, in the new manner, separate accommodation for the family away from their retainers.

In 1277 the King decreed that wool could only be bought and sold in the county towns and hence Shrewsbury attained the enormous commercial advantage of being a 'staple town', that is, one of the eleven official exchanges for the wool trade. This rule brought revenue to the Crown and increased the town's prosperity, concentrating economic power in the hands of the merchant families.

Buyers from Italy and the Netherlands were now compelled to do business here rather than directly with producers in the countryside. Much of the raw wool (and, later, cloth) originating in Shropshire and the adjoining Welsh counties was exported, mostly to Flanders. Shrewsbury played its part on this European stage, and English merchants were now trading with countries as far afield as the Mediterranean: spices, glass vessels and decorative pottery, iron, oil and textiles were coming here in quantity from Spain and Italy. Shops of the time stocked Italian silk, Flemish linen, leather goods from Cordoba and steel from Germany.

One example of a Shrewsbury businessman who achieved international stature was Nicholas de Ludlow (this surname came from his extensive commercial interests in that town). In state documents surviving from 1278 he is described as 'king's merchant' and recorded as being paid more than £2,000 by dealers in Flanders. This country was the main importer of English wool and Nicholas had dealings with the mayors of Ypres, Ghent, St Omer and Bruges.

In 1305 another merchant, Richard Stury, was appointed by Edward I to go to Antwerp, representing English interests in negotiations with the Duke of Brabant over the establishment of a trading base there. Both John of Ludlow and Richard Stury are known to have possessed hangings, possibly tapestries, made in Rheims.

In spite of the fact that reliable preservative methods had not been developed, wine was imported from the English province of Gascony, generally via Bristol, to be widely consumed by the better-off. For most, though, a light ale was the main daily drink; in towns, of course, the water was often polluted. Records show that brewing was a trade commonly practised by women, generally those who were widows or unmarried.

Women who had helped with their husbands' trades were often able to carry on as widows. In 1297, for example, tax records show that Juliana, the widow of Peter the Potter (a surname which covered metalworking as well as the production of pottery) was taxed on her possession of a piece of important technical equipment – a mould for brass-making. After his death both she and her son William were taxed as independent operators; she evidently continued in business in her own right. Extant tax records for this family cover forty-five years. At the higher end of the social scale only one woman, Isabel Borrey, the wife of John of Ludlow, is recorded as the commercial equal of her husband and a burgess in her own right.

The thirteenth century was the heyday for wool traders from Shrewsbury and Ludlow, who were among England's most powerful entrepreneurs. Large numbers of people were employed in the related trades such as fulling, dyeing and weaving.

Stokesay Castle, built by the merchant Laurence of Ludlow, in the 1270s. In spite of the name, Laurence was a member of the leading wool-trading family of Shrewsbury. This building, which he was given a licence to crenellate (effectively, to fortify) in 1291, demonstrates his aspirations.

Disease and Decline

Ultimately, the health and wealth of the nation had to depend on its ability to produce food – which could not always be relied upon. The years 1316–17 brought crop failure and famine to the whole country, and after this disaster areas of poor soil were gradually abandoned. The result, as always, was that settlement congregated around the major urban areas and many small villages were deserted. Political instability and war preceded the death of Edward II, who visited the town in 1322.

The outbreaks of plague had taken their toll and a huge fire gutted large parts of Wyle Cop in 1393. Rebuilding appears to have taken more than twenty years. Nevertheless, some of the town's most substantial, prestigious and long-lasting timber buildings date from this period.

Around the middle of the fourteenth century, a competitive cloth industry finally developed in Wales, and Shrewsbury's role as a market and supply centre for the marches seems to have been transferred to Oswestry, Welshpool and Bishop's Castle. Whilst the leading Shrewsbury merchants managed to maintain a presence in Coventry, the great cloth centre of the midlands, lesser men were soon ousted and Shrewsbury was no longer represented in the great European textile centres as it had once been. Its business was increasingly in the production, rather than the distribution, of cloth.

Tudor Shrewsbury

However, the accession to the throne of Henry Tudor at the end of the Wars of the Roses in 1485 ushered in a period of peace and relative prosperity throughout the country. This was no less so for Shrewsbury, where new trades developed to support the town. Most of the great timber-framed houses of Shrewsbury date from the Tudor period; many merchants built houses with a view to letting them.

The Black Death

In 1348–39, in 1361 and again seven years later, the epidemic now known as the Black Death swept England, and between a third and half the population was annihilated by it. Shrewsbury's population declined by about a third in the century after 1377, and the early part of the fifteenth century seems to have been economically disastrous for the town with a decline in trade of 70 per cent. One result of this demographic change was a weakening of the feudal system and hence greater emancipation for peasants, who could sell their labour to the highest bidder.

We now know that this, the pneumonic plague, was spread through droplets to the lungs, but medical knowledge then was minimal. Although the religious houses could offer little more than spiritual consolation, they were often the only form of help available to the stricken. These 'hospitals' specialised in providing care for the sick and old. In the later medieval period some became almshouses, providing accommodation, based on endowments from the wealthy.

The School

One important new element introduced into the town during the Tudor period was the Free Grammar School, founded by a charter of the boy-king Edward VI in 1552. The School was to be governed by rules agreed between the town's Corporation and the Bishop of Lichfield. The new establishment filled a gap left by the dissolution of the Abbey, which would almost certainly have provided for the educational needs of boys in the town. Funding came from the revenues of the old monastic establishments of St Mary's and St Chad's, these having been dissolved. Royal patronage for the Free Grammar School attracted local money and pupils. The first list extant names 266 boys – a huge number for the time. The School's extensive facilities were rivalled only by Eton and Winchester.

Between 1589 and 1630, in tune with Shrewsbury's prosperity in these years, further building was undertaken, providing the main wing in 1595 and the teaching block in 1630 adjoining the oldest timber-

The School building.

The main entrance to the Free Grammar School, with its engaging stone figures, expresses, in Greek, Renaissance ideals of learning. One student is Polymathes – one who knows much; the other is Philomathes – one who wants to learn!

framed section, the medieval Riggs Hall. A further house, still standing, was built a few miles north of the town at Grinshill, where pupils could be evacuated during outbreaks of plague. As with other schools of the period, the curriculum focused on the teaching of Latin, without which no educated man could achieve success, since all legal and commercial transactions were conducted in this language. Astronomy and astrology, as well as some geography, were taught, and mathematics became a feature. The School's first headmaster,

Sir Philip Sidney

Shrewsbury's famous School, granted a Royal charter by King Edward VI in 1552, has introduced many interesting and talented figures to the world during its long history. An early scholar was Sir Philip Sydney, (1554–1586) a glamorous member of Elizabeth I's Court – poet, diplomat and soldier – who died young, from wounds sustained at Zutphen in the Netherlands in a campaign against Spanish control of the region. Sidney was the son of the President of the Council of the March, which met in Ludlow, and as a schoolboy he stayed at the Council of the Marches, opposite the School's building.

The young Philip Sidney and his brother Robert.

Thomas Ashton, was a cultivated and saintly man with links to the court intelligentsia. A manuscript of the religious plays he produced here remains in the School's library, an institution which has always been a source of justifiable pride. In 1687 the library added to a collection of seventeenth-century books with the purchase of a copy of Sir Isaac Newton's great work *Principia Mathematica*.

The Later Wool Trade

In parallel with the expansion of the School, a renewed trade in wool was developing in the later sixteenth century. An Act of Parliament gave the Drapers' Company of Shrewsbury a monopoly of the finishing and distribution of cloth woven on the farms of Wales. This marked a major shift in the kind of work done in the town towards production techniques. 'Finishing' involved cutting off the rough nap

and was done in the workshops of master shearmen, of whom there were eighty-one in 1553. Thirty years later their number had expanded further and they contributed substantially to the economy. The cloth, not of high quality, sold widely and was exported to the Continent to make working garments.

The Drapers' Hall, built in the 1570s and 1580s, where the Company's affairs were administered. Inside, original items of furniture made for the building can still be seen.

Portraits of Thomas Jones and his wife Sarah. This leading Shrewsbury lawyer was Bailiff six times, High Sheriff of Shropshire in 1624 and Chief Magistrate and Mayor in 1638, and he thus epitomises the status to which the merchant class could aspire. He is mentioned in the Charter of that year, which gave Shrewsbury this new dignity of a mayor, replacing the two bailiffs. Thomas Jones's robes are probably those of a bailiff, and his wife, the daughter of a Chester mayor, is also richly dressed. The couple, painted in 1615, are depicted in their early forties. The Jones' mansion is now part of the Prince Rupert Hotel.

By the beginning of the seventeenth century the Drapers' Company was the most powerful single body in Shrewsbury, counting within its ranks the wealthiest burgesses. The Mercers' and Shearmen's Companies helped the trade to flourish by creating competition.

The population of Shrewsbury grew rapidly and by 1640 it was seven thousand. This expansion was reflected in commerce: in 1600 so much traffic was using the approach road by the Abbey that, according to local residents, it was being worn away. Records also show an immense rise in litigation, mostly relating to the financial affairs of gentry and yeomen farmers from the rural hinterland. Shrewsbury was now a financial centre where you could borrow and lend money.

Politics

The relationship between town and Crown remained somewhat tense until the late seventeenth century, and after his restoration to the throne Charles II attempted to bring local government under tighter control by removing the town's right to have a mayor. Seventeenth-century charters seem to have come and gone in this way, reflecting the political manoeuvrings of the Stuart kings. The old charter was finally restored in 1688, just before the accession of William and Mary.

Partly as a result of the role of certain powerful aristocrats in bringing William and Mary to the throne, politics in the eighteenth century were dominated by this group. Their landowning interests and the power they exercised over their tenants gave them control of seats in Parliament, where a series of great Shropshire dynasties, including the Bradford family and the Hills of Hawkstone, battled it out amongst themselves for such seats and for offices like that of Lord Lieutenant.

By the early years of the nineteenth century the middle class were increasingly dissatisfied with the grip on government held by the aristocracy. In 1835 the Municipal Corporation Act reformed borough councils and updated their constitutions, dissolving the ancient trade guilds which had long been an anachronistic feature of local government. Gradually

The image of Charles II, from his Charter.

the franchise was extended, although bribery remained a feature of elections when Disraeli was first elected to Parliament, for Shrewsbury, in 1841.

Industry

Like the other towns of the Welsh march, Shrewsbury lay at the heart of a busy network of rural industry, especially that derived from water power. The hilly landscape and profusion of streams encouraged watermills, and it is now believed that the Shropshire landscape was continuously exploited for charcoal burning, perhaps even from pre-historic times. Charcoal was an essential ingredient in the processes of glass- as well as pottery-making, and it was also required for lime production. Burnt lime was extensively used in agriculture and building, and recent discoveries have revealed a vast number of forgotten limekilns.

Lords Lieutenant and Nabobs

Politics remained in the hands of the upper class, and after 1737 contested elections were considered an unnecessary expense. Like all British aristocrats, the Shropshire grandees, while they might maintain a house in the county town, were firmly based on their landed estates. Their prized office was that of Lord Lieutenant of the county. During the early part of the century the most important of the Shropshire political grandees was Henry Newport, third Earl of Bradford. He was followed as Lord Lieutenant in 1760 by the faintly sinister figure of William Pulteney, whose acquisition of some of the Bradford lands was a source of bitter political satire: 'A brilliant, vindictive, mean man.'

H. A. Herbert of Oakley Park had the office in 1735 and went on to become Lord Herbert of Chirbury and Earl of Powis in 1748. Concerned largely to benefit his own social and political group, this aristocrat generally kept out of Shrewsbury's affairs but was nonetheless criticised for attempting to secure an official post in the town for his nominee. 'Lord Powis is more absolute in this part of the world,' complained an opponent, 'than the King of France is in his capital city.'

Like other powerful men returning laden with wealth from adventures in India – where they gained the title of Nabob – Robert Clive dominated the political scene in the county town in the 1770s.

The English Bridge by Edward Dayes, in 1804. This view shows a waterwheel which drew water from the river for the town centre's water supply.

At Atcham there was a watermill driven by the River Tern in the thirteenth century and there were several mills working in Shrewsbury, for fulling (part of the process of cloth manufacture) and to grind corn. The Abbey controlled these, and this gave the monks a monopoly of flour production. Naturally, such an economic advantage was resented by the town's merchants until they established their own mills, operated by horsepower, and a windmill.

The presence of the river, combined with substantial woodland around the town, provided the raw materials necessary to produce leather. Hence tanneries became a major feature of the medieval town. Water was a vital resource in this business, and there were tanneries all along the river and the watercourses leading to it, particularly in the damp marshy area that is now Barker Street. This industry relied heavily on dog faeces and urine for the curing process, and its raw material of animal hides cannot have diminished the unpleasantness for those living nearby. Consequently, those parts of the river where this work flourished tended to be shunned by wealthier residents and to become haunts of vice and violence. Tanneries continued to exist close to the Welsh Bridge well into the twentieth century, although by this time means had been found to control offensive smells.

During the fourteenth century the declining wool trade made way for more local crafts dependent on the production of leather. Both men and women found work in this trade, women dealing with fur trimmings and the lighter, more intricate tasks. The pelts of rabbits, squirrels, foxes and lambs were used to trim the garments of such local people as could afford them, including those of merchant and gentry status from the wider hinterland. Virtually everything that a gentleman or lady might require, from needlework items to horse-riding accessories, were made in the town. As already noted, stock inventories of shops of the time reveal a staggering range of imported luxury goods, although all the humbler necessities of life, such as building materials, furniture, kitchen equipment and textiles, were of course produced locally.

Metalworking was an important industry, its furnaces located for safety across the river at Coleham. Ironworking, later associated famously with the Ironbridge Gorge, always developed in medieval times near rivers as it required water for washing the ore and water power to work the mighty bellows and hammers of the forges. Furnaces are known to have existed at Shifnal and Cleobury Mortimer in 1562, and by 1717 there were no fewer than fifteen forges along the Tern Valley, including one at Atcham.

All was to change in the middle of the eighteenth century with Abraham Darby's discovery of a method of smelting iron using coke, instead of the more costly charcoal, and henceforward this industry was concentrated in the Severn Gorge.

Linen
Rural Shropshire in the seventeenth and eighteenth centuries had a thriving linen industry, based on small farms where a field would be

given over to growing flax. The best-quality fibres were made into linen, the remainder making rope and sacks. The government offered subsidies to small farmers, whose wives were expected to maintain fields of flax. The work of dressing hemp was assigned to prisoners at the gaol – who complained in 1714 about the dusty conditions it entailed. Many households were involved with the business, and the existence of a skilled workforce was a factor in the development of flax mills in the town.

Industrialisation, however, was on the way: in 1788 an entrepreneur from Leeds built a mill for flax-spinning and two Shrewsbury brothers, Benjamin and Thomas Benyon, joined him later. Following a fire, the Benyons brought in a local surveyor, Charles Bage, who designed an extraordinarily forward-looking cast-iron structure for the new mill.

North of the town, set back from the A49, stands the pioneering Ditherington Flax Mill of about 1797, the first building ever to have a cast-iron skeleton structure. Housing was provided here, for several hundred people, employees and their families and young apprentices. The building later became a maltings.

Thomas Telford

The modern town of Telford records the name of the great engineer Thomas Telford (1757–1834), but his early work was carried out in Shrewsbury, where he arrived in 1787. It was William Pulteney MP who was responsible for bringing his fellow-Scot to

Shropshire when he commissioned Telford to convert the Castle into a home in 1789. Telford was the architect of several Shropshire churches and was called in to advise the authorities about the condition of the tower of Old St Chad's church. He foresaw the tower's imminent collapse, but because he appeared to lack experience his wise advice was ignored. Nevertheless, the young engineer's star rose rapidly and he was soon County Surveyor and the engineer for the Shrewsbury and Ellesmere Canal.

The cast iron for the new Flax Mill was produced in Shrewsbury by Telford's associate, William Hazledine. A successful ironmaster, Hazledine became Mayor and had amassed a large fortune by the time of his death in 1840. Remains of his factory still stand, close to the Coleham pumping station. Many of Telford's great engineering projects, such as the Menai Bridge, made use of ironwork supplied by Hazledine.

RELIGION AND CHURCH LIFE

*'He gave the whole suburb which is without the East Gate to the blessed
Peter, Prince of Apostles.'*
—The Norman chronicler Ordericus Vitalis

MEDIEVAL England was dominated by the practice and beliefs of Christianity. The priesthood maintained a monopoly on education and literacy and was extremely powerful socially, commercially and politically. There was only one nunnery in the county, the White Ladies priory of Augustinian canonesses established in 1186 at St Leonard's, Brewood, but there were twelve monasteries, all led by Earl Roger's abbeys of Shrewsbury and Much Wenlock. Shrewsbury Abbey housed members of the

Magnificent arcading at Wenlock Priory.

Small rural settlements also required churches, and the Heath Chapel, in its evocatively lonely setting in the Corve Dale, is a perfect example of a small-scale Norman religious building.

Benedictine order but the Cluniac Much Wenlock, with its religious allegiance to a mother house in the Loire valley, was the larger institution. Its great church, 350 feet long, was the largest in the county and its community numbered about forty monks. Monks were involved in most aspects of life and, as landowners, were responsible for agriculture and for pushing back the frontiers of cultivated land. Shrewsbury Abbey was involved with fisheries and mills.

During the twelfth and thirteenth centuries, however, great changes took place in the ecclesiastical order, in particular the organisation and status of the priesthood – changes that made an impact on society.

The Friars

Anglo-Saxon priests were often married, and passed their benefices, regarded as private property, on to their sons. Eventually this led to a degradation of the office and a lack of respect for the clergy. As a result, by about 1200 a quarter of England's parish churches had been taken over either by bishops or by monastic institutions, but the great religious houses which developed in this way, with their huge wealth, political interests and landholdings, came in their turn to look increasingly worldly, even corrupt.

Concurrently, larger urban centres were developing for the first time since the Roman Empire, focused on new industries like textile production. These cities attracted large numbers of poor rural workers, who settled in shanty towns outside their walls. Existing churches in the old urban framework found themselves unable to cope with these large numbers. New religious orders, of friars (brothers) dedicated to poverty and following the charismatic example of St Francis of Assisi (1182–1226), stepped into the void, building large new churches and ministering to those on the fringes of society, largely through the medium of emotional preaching. This was a time of new religious fervour in Europe, stimulated by the depredations of the plague. The immediacy and personal quality of preaching made it a hugely important form of communication that entailed the need for large open churches with good acoustics.

The remains of the Franciscan Friary of St Julian .

Lady Hawise de Powis, wife of Sir John de Charlton, was a bene-factress of the Franciscan Friary. This is her seal, c.1320 (reversed photograph of the seal matrix).

These new European movements adhered literally to the vow of poverty and their members chose sites on the edges of existing towns, often outside the walls among the dispossessed poor. The first to arrive in England, in 1221, were members of the order founded by St Dominic – the Blackfriars. In 1232 the Dominicans established a house on the steep slope down to the River Severn near St Mary's Water Lane. They were followed ten years later by the Franciscans, or Greyfriars, who settled just outside the walls of Shrewsbury with the generous assistance of Henry III. In 1254 a third group, the Austin (Augustinian) friars, arrived, at the site now occupied by Shrewsbury Sixth Form College. Prominent local people gave grants and donations; the wealthy merchant William Vaughan (the remains of whose mansion can be seen inside the present Music Hall building) gave generously to St John's Hospital and to Haughmond Abbey as well as to the Austin Friars.

The friars were evangelical, accommodating large congregations in their churches as well as travelling to preach in the surrounding countryside. Although not priests, they were frequently asked to become confessors to wealthy families and through such influence brought about a greater charitable awareness of the poor.

The universal belief in the afterlife led most wealthy people to found, or endow, monastic houses where those dedicated to the religious life would pray for the souls of their patrons and their families. Following the example of his leader, William the Conqueror, Earl Roger founded Shrewsbury Abbey, and before his death in 1094 he did his best to assure his entry to heaven, after a life of ruthless military conquest, by taking monastic vows here.

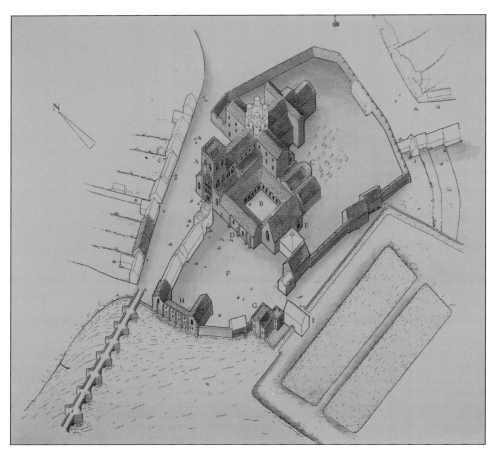

Shrewsbury Abbey: an imaginative reconstruction of its appearance in the fifteenth century.

Roger's patronage established the Abbey on very secure foundations. As mentioned elsewhere in this book, he granted to it the new suburb to the east of the town, Abbey Foregate, and rents from this independent community were an additional source of revenue. Because the Abbey operated as a business, its entrepreneurial approach both benefited and caused friction with the town's merchants. Commercially the Abbey's site was magnificent, offering control over the river crossing to the town and therefore all approaching traders. In addition, it had three extremely profitable watermills which had a monopoly on the supply of grain to the town. Although only a small community (twelve monks in 1460), the Abbey was a substantial property owner, letting and selling to support its religious and charitable activities, including care of the poor

However, by the early part of the twelfth century the town of Shrewsbury had expanded into the new suburbs of Coton, Castle Foregate and Coleham, the last close to the Abbey. The increasing population and commercial strength of the town led to conflict with the economic expectations of the monks. An uneasy peace existed between town and Abbey over milling rights, and it was a cause of annoyance to townsfolk that the Abbey had the right to run a three-day fair – a huge source of revenue. By 1267, however, the town had been granted the right to hold its own two fairs.

The Church was the focus of charity, providing virtually the only safety net for the poor, the old and the sick. It also offered help in the afterlife through prayers for the souls of the dead. Those who could afford to do so set up chantries – generally altars or private chapels within a church where priests were paid to say mass for the souls of the dead. This was the purpose of the collegiate church (home to a group of priests) at Battlefield, established to pray for those killed in the Battle of Shrewsbury.

The Break with Rome and the End of the Monasteries

The Christian Church has been subject to waves of evangelism throughout its history. The idea that ordinary people might have access to the gospels in

This glass panel from Pulley Old Hall (now demolished) shows a familiar harvest scene. According to the tithe system, which prevailed throughout the country, a tenth of all agricultural and other produce had to be given to the church. The economic value of tithes made it a good move financially for monks to appropriate parish churches, which had their own incomes.

their own languages was crucial to the new religious consciousness sweeping Europe in the fourteenth century. The Englishman John Wycliffe (c. 1320–1384) has been called 'the morning star of the Reformation' because of his translation of the Bible, a process which many years later resulted in English replacing Latin and French as the official language of the Church. His followers, the Lollards, succeeded in weaving a puritan element into English Christianity that gained strength two hundred years later. However, the earliest manifestation of what we now call the Reformation actually occurred in Bohemia in the fifteenth century, under the religious leadership of John Hus. He attacked abuses in the Church and emphasised the absolute authority of the Bible.

However, no serious breakaway from the authority of Rome over European Christendom occurred until the time of the German Augustinian monk, Martin Luther. Orthodox Christians believed that, after death, the human soul would experience a period of purging of sin (Purgatory) before being united with God in heaven. Luther at-

The End of Shrewsbury's Monasteries

In Shrewsbury, the Abbey had been mismanaged for some time, accruing debts and not maintaining proper accounting procedures. In 1536 rain was found to be pouring in through the choir roof and the Abbot was accused of failing to maintain its buildings adequately. Three years later the King sent four commissioners to demand the handover of the Abbey and all its assets to his authority. There was little the Abbot, Thomas Botelar, and his seventeen monks could do but bow before the inevitable. All were pensioned off.

In 1546 speculators snapped up the building complex and sold it on immediately to a Shrewsbury businessman, William Langley. He converted parts of it to a private residence for himself, known as the Abbey Mansion, and the original refectory pulpit, dating from the 1330s, still stands in what were the Abbey Gardens.

At the Augustinian Friary there was an outright scandal. There were only two friars, both Irish, and the house contained no food, no drink and no bedding. The Prior, described as 'a man like to be in a frenzy' was found to be selling off everything as fast as he could!

This mid-eighteenth-century view shows parts of the Abbey building that survived sixteenth-century demolitions. Sadly, more of this was to go when Telford improved the road to Holyhead a century later. The remaining gable end that can be seen today forms the headquarters of the Shropshire Wildlife Trust.

tacked the widespread practice of selling 'indulgences' by which an individual could buy himself out of some of this penitential time. By 1520 Luther's ideas, many drawing inspiration from the humanist New Learning of the Renaissance, had crystallised. He came to believe that Rome was in error. Within the next five years Luther's ideas had been accepted in many German cities, initially with huge appeal to the craft guilds, and they were finally adopted by the princely families.

In England, though, the separation of the Church from its historic headquarters in Rome was political and dynastic rather than theological. King Henry VIII had failed to secure the all-important male heir with his wife, Katharine of Aragon, and now wished to marry another woman. Frustrated by the Pope in his attempts to divorce the Spanish queen, Henry decided to declare himself head of the English

Church, incorporating into the new institution certain (but not many) Protestant ideas. These ideas tended to focus on dislike of a foreign pope and envy of the wealth of the Church. The king himself remained in spirit a Catholic until his death in 1547, although he chose Protestant scholars to educate his son Edward.

Henry's separation of the English Church from Rome was formalised with the Dissolution of the Monasteries. This move is now seen by historians as a cynical attempt to remove the wealth of these bodies to the Crown, although it did have the effect of redistributing money and land to the ambitious and intelligent middle-class men who were Henry's loyal functionaries.

Many monastic buildings were sold off to lawyers and court officials shrewd enough to see the speculative advantages to be gleaned from all this newly available property. Unwanted buildings fell into disrepair, and in some cases their charitable functions were taken over by mercantile organisations. When the inhabitants of the various houses realised that dissolution was inevitable, many of them accepted retirement on modest pensions. Some became parish priests in their own locality.

Pilgrimage, Festivals and Shows

During the Middle Ages an important source of revenue for an ecclesiastical foundation could be the possession of a relic, often part of the body of a saint, with its capacity to attract hordes of the faithful. The most famous example of medieval pilgrimage to the shrine of a saint is that of St Thomas Becket at Canterbury, celebrated in the poet Chaucer's *Canterbury Tales*. Pilgrimages brought immense revenue to towns like Canterbury, and other places sought to emulate this commercial success. During the 1130s the monks of Shrewsbury were much concerned about their lack of such a crowd-puller. An apparent miracle convinced them that the Welsh virgin-martyr, Saint Winefred, of Holywell near St Asaph in north Wales, must be their

Every trade had its own decorated arbour. This picture shows the original stone arch of the Shoemakers' Arbour, dating from 1679, and recently reset at the Dingle in the Quarry Park.

patroness, and an expedition to dig up her body and bring it to Shrewsbury was mounted forthwith. This extraordinary operation was completed in 1138 and a shrine to the saint was established. Such was its evident popularity that in the fourteenth century the shrine was refurbished and brought up to date in style. In 1487 Abbot Thomas Mynde set up a popular guild for the wealthiest Shrewsbury citizens and their wives in Saint Winefred's honour. Recent excavation at the Abbey has confirmed ambitious rebuilding at the point when the cult was most ardently followed, so it is likely that the Abbey benefited financially from the large numbers of pilgrims that allegedly miraculous relics could attract.

Medieval life provided a largely illiterate populace with plenty of imaginative outlets in the colour, music and drama of Church festivals. Particularly important and spectacular were the rites associated with the feast of Corpus Christi, on the Thursday after Trinity Sunday. This early summer festival was marked with a great procession by the craft fellowships dressed in their liveries and carrying candles and banners. The monstrance, a decorated casket displaying the consecrated wafer believed to be the body of Christ, was carried behind by the priest, beneath a canopy held aloft by four acolytes. The procession ended across the river at Kingsland, where each guild had its own booth, or arbour, for eating, drinking and dancing. It was an occasion for merrymaking and cordiality and even the Abbot and his senior colleagues enjoyed a drink with leading merchants. This practice led, at the beginning of the 1590s, to the development of what is known as the Old Shrewsbury Show.

Between 1564 and 1606, however, as Protestant influence grew, the craft fellowships began to take a more austere tone, banning what were deemed to be superstitious practices. In its place they initiated a secular parade, although this too attracted similar criticism.

After the Dissolution

Following Henry VIII's break with Rome all church services were conducted in English, but the gains from this greater public access to the rites of religion were soon to be offset by the iconoclastic vandalism of reformers. It is now known that a huge amount of religious art was wantonly destroyed. In the 1580s, for example, glass was taken from St Mary's and stone crosses were destroyed. Under the stern jurisdiction of the puritan preacher John Tomkys, who came here from Bilston in Staffordshire, the inside of St Mary's was whitewashed and painted with the Ten Commandments. Tomkys was certainly a bigot, but he was not ignorant of European Protestant ideas: he had published a catechism on the Lord's Prayer and translated books by a Swiss reformer.

Protestantism gained a stronger foothold in this country as a result of the persecutions of Henry's Catholic daughter, Queen Mary, who was half-Spanish and had married the Spanish king. By the end of her reign it had a warm following in Shrewsbury and continued to be influential until the Civil War and beyond.

The great majority of the population now adhered to the new Church of England, with its reduced ritual and absence of religious information in the form of statues and imagery. Combined with the new climate of moral and spiritual fervour, this change created once more a need for better quality and more extensive preaching. In Shrewsbury, as elsewhere, the burgesses employed a public preacher, in this case the vicar of St Mary's. His sermons became a matter for civic pride, and such was the interest that ministers from surrounding areas assembled to give lectures, known as 'exercises', in informal competition with one another. By 1600, too, puritan feeling in Shrewsbury is evident in the marked increase in records of penalties imposed for sexual offences.

Thomas Ashton, the first headmaster of Shrewsbury School, was an educator of great saintliness in the Cambridge humanist tradition. During the years after his arrival in 1561 he produced three religious plays.

During the seventeenth century Shrewsbury was home to several dissenting groups, not least the Presbyterians, led by the fiery vicars of St Chad's and St Mary's, Francis Tallents and John Bryan. After the Restoration of Charles II there was less tolerance of the extremes of puritanism and its proponents became suspect. Tallents and Bryan both lost their jobs as a result of an Act of Parliament aimed at purging the Anglican church of puritans, perhaps because they were sus-

The remarkable Samuel Lee (1783–1852), who rose from being a humble Shropshire farm lad to become Professor of Hebrew at Cambridge. Until 1871 all university lecturers were ordained in the Anglican ministry, and the artist, Richard Evans, shows his sitter in this role.

pected of anti-Royalist sentiments. By 1715, though, Presbyterians formed the largest dissenting group in Shrewsbury, with a congregation of four hundred; but they were not universally popular, as is demonstrated by the fact that during the summer of that year there was an outbreak of severe rioting against dissenters right across the county. The Oswestry meeting house was vandalised and those of Wem, Whitchurch and Shrewsbury were completely destroyed. These attacks coincide with a renewal of interest in the deposed Stuart monarchy and the first abortive rebellion, in 1715, of the Roman Catholic James Stuart; evidently there was some Shropshire sympathy for the Jacobite cause.

This was another period of renewed spiritual fervour when three of the churches in the town centre were re-built (including St Alkmund's, with its cast-iron windows). The eighteenth century witnessed the growth of what was to become the most influential new denomination, the Wesleyan Methodists. Like the reform movement instituted five hundred years earlier by the Friars, this fed on the needs of the urban poor. By 1744 there was a congregation of Methodists in Shrewsbury and it was visited seventeen years later by John Wesley himself, who opened their first purpose-built chapel. The Baptists, too, enjoyed a period of expansion under the leadership of their preacher, 'John the Baptist' Palmer.

Apart from some well-established dissenting families, such as the Quaker Darbys of Coalbrookdale, most dissenters were working-class and did not have the resources to build grandly. Hence their chapels tended to be unassuming. A hundred years after the rioting, though, and following the huge development of industry during that period, the scene was very different and there were no fewer than eleven chapels, of various dissenting creeds, in Shrewsbury. Several of these had schools attached, and until 1818 Charles Darwin himself attended the one in Claremont Hill that was the home of Dr Case, minister of the Unitarian chapel on the High Street. In 1832 the Welsh Independent Methodists were confident enough to erect an imposing stone tabernacle in a prominent position on Dogpole.

Philanthropy

One group which came to make an immense contribution to the life of the nation, paradoxically through their exclusion from many avenues of public life, was the Quakers. Unlike other groups, they made

little effort to conceal their religious allegiance, were harassed by the borough authorities and eventually concentrated in the Ironbridge area. However, by 1691–92 they were able to license a meeting house and burial ground on St John's Hill.

The classical elegance of this chapel on Town Walls demonstrates the confidence of a Nonconformist community in 1834.

The original Salop Infirmary. In 1830 this building was replaced by the present handsome design, by Edward Haycock, which in the 1980s was converted into sought-after apartments and a small shopping complex.

Their numbers declined, although powerful individuals continued to make an impact. Mrs Abiah Darby, for example, of the famous Ironbridge family, was confident enough to express her concern repeatedly in the 1750s about drunkenness and general immorality in Shrewsbury. As the eighteenth century progressed, the intelligence, application and business acumen of many Quaker families became a major motivating factor of the Industrial Revolution.

Some of the business community's energy manifested itself in social reform and philanthropy. In 1745 leading burgesses combined to fund the Salop Infirmary near St Mary's church. The honorary post of Treasurer to this institution carried considerable prestige and was occupied in turn by members of the county's leading families.

Four years later, following the medieval charitable tradition, an elegant almshouse building was erected on the Mount, close to the Welsh Bridge. This was provided by the generosity of a Shrewsbury draper, James Millington, whose brother John had earlier provided scholarships to Cambridge for poor boys of Shrewsbury School. The new prison was designed by Edward Haycock in conjunction with Telford on the lines suggested by the penal reformer John Howard, whose bust surmounts the great entrance portico.

In 1798 the poet Samuel Taylor Coleridge, intending to follow a career as a minister, came to Shrewsbury to preach, his sermon inspiring a young resident of Wem, William Hazlitt, who later became an admired essayist. For Coleridge, however, history intervened in the shape of an annuity which allowed him to forsake the religious for the poetic calling.

Roman Catholics

Since Henry VIII's break with Rome, and following the persecution of Protestants by his daughter Mary, there had been considerable hostility in the country to Roman Catholics, who were felt to have divided loyalties. In Shropshire a number of old Catholic families had survived, and in the eighteenth century there were known to be seven

Julia Bainbridge Wightman (1815–1898)

The wife of the Vicar of St Alkmund's was a national figure in the Temperance movement at a time when alcohol addiction was a scourge, particularly of the industrial poor. A deeply religious woman with a developed social conscience, she first sought to help young females who had been drawn into prostitution. Later she became aware of the widespread social damage being caused by alcohol. This change of direction followed a series of references in her diary to becoming 'tipsy' herself! She was responsible for the building of the Working Men's Hall in The Square and organised outings to the countryside to tempt people away from the Shrewsbury Show, then considered an incitement to drunkenness. The home which she shared with her husband Charles, close to St Alkmund's, was extended to include a 'mission room'.

Julia's Wightman's home, in the late Victorian Tudor style.

Roman Catholic chapels in private homes in Shrewsbury but only one that was public. Legal emancipation for Roman Catholics did not come until 1829, and even then it was nearly thirty years before Shrewsbury's Catholic community acquired its own cathedral. This was designed in an authentic Gothic mode by the son of the famous promoter of that style, Augustus Welby Pugin. Shropshire Catholics were fortunate in the patronage of the devout and extremely wealthy Earl of Shrewsbury, who, even though he did not live in the county, lavished some his vast fortune on church building. The cathedral is thus a grand and lofty structure, unlike its equivalents elsewhere.

The Anglican community, however, has not acquired a cathedral, in spite of having an appropriate building in the Abbey, which remains a parish church. The magnificent rotunda of St Chad's functions as the civic church, and other town centre churches have been declared redundant, including the very beautiful St Mary's, which is now used for concerts.

6   THE CIVIL WAR

T HE ENGLISH Civil War had complex causes involving all three kingdoms – England, Scotland and Ireland. At the centre of the dispute between King and Parliament lay the unshakable belief of King Charles I (1600–1649) in his God-given authority to rule and his consequent ambition to establish absolute personal power. Against this was ranged an élite group composed of members of the mercantile and gentry classes. These men were determined to resist the King's aims, in defence of their own economic and political autonomy. They saw themselves as the defenders of ancient freedoms dating back to Magna Carta when the barons forced the King to accept demands for greater autonomy. In addition, at a time when religion remained intimately connected to national identity, the nonconformist Scots, and many English people, maintained a strong distaste for the Church of Rome. This had developed in certain areas into an extreme Protestantism, tinged with new republican ideas. Along with other attempts to centralise government, Charles insisted

The Gatehouse of the Shrewsbury base of the Council of the March. Built in 1620 during James I's reign, it shows a characteristically Jacobean range of ornament derived from classical tradition, columns and a pediment.

The Council House itself is the less spectacular building opposite the Gatehouse. This is a Victorian view of the interior.

on an orthodox Anglicanism seen by many as tainted with popery. Hence a wide spectrum of classes and political opinion rallied under the banner of Parliament against the threat of royal despotism.

The midlands played a key role in the Civil War. It was the arena for many key battles, and its inhabitants suffered greatly from the depredations of the soldiery of both sides. Because of the town's strategic position in the centre of the country, Charles chose to raise his standard at Nottingham, which he did on 22 August 1642. This was a traditional signal for his supporters to rally, and from here, hoping to raise money and armed support all the way, he advanced across the region, riding via Derby to Wellington, and then to Shrewsbury, where the Castle had already been hastily refurbished for military purposes. The king entered the town on 20 September and took up lodgings in the Council House, opposite the Castle. He remained there until December.

Sympathies in Shropshire began to shift with the arrival of the King. Unfortunately for the royal cause, the behaviour of the troops lacked discipline and there were numerous complaints of looting and worse, right across the region. The reputation of the King's nephew, Prince Rupert, a gifted military leader, is gravely tarnished by his failure to control this behaviour, and the relatively unsophisticated inhabitants of Shrewsbury, hitherto loyal to the King for traditional reasons, were to be severely tested during Rupert's stay in the town. To add insult to injury, Shrewsbury was an important link in the King's chain of support extending across Wales to Ireland and the townsfolk were asked to pay for upgrading its defences once more. There is little doubt that puritan sympathies, combined with irritation at having to house Royalist soldiery, led to an ambivalence which threatened security. It was perhaps inevitable that the Royalist garrison housed in the Castle was finally betrayed.

Charles was chronically short of money, and the fact that the troops were not paid properly was a further inducement to plundering the hapless households with which they were billeted. A letter of complaint to Sir Francis Ottley, military governor of Shrewsbury, survives alleging repeated looting and violence. The victim, John Weever, makes a point of saying that he and other sufferers at the hands of the troops are 'most dutifull subjects to his majestie'.

Prince Rupert of the Rhine, the King's nephew, who lodged whilst in Shrewsbury at what is now the Prince Rupert Hotel.

> ### The Mint Revived
>
> The King's financial difficulties were partly alleviated by the relocation of the Royal Mint from Aberystwyth to Shrewsbury. Under the superintendence of Thomas Bushell, a businessman from Evesham, coinage to pay the soldiery was produced from melted-down plate sent to the King by the colleges of Oxford and Cambridge, and by local families. However, the Mint was finally not much help, unable as it was to produce more than a thousand pounds a week (nonetheless a gigantic sum for that period), and it was moved away after a couple of months. The King was reduced to selling titles: a Shropshire knight is reported as buying a peerage for a sum between £2,000 and £10,000!

The political position in Shrewsbury at the time of Charles's visit in itself demonstrates the internecine quality of the conflict. Of the town's two MPs, one was Royalist and the other Parliamentarian. Parliament had sympathisers throughout Shropshire, while Shrewsbury, like other places with existing defences, was held by Royalists. Both sides made serious attempts to raise money for their cause. In February 1643 Parliament had established County Committees manned by local dignitaries. The Shropshire Committee consisted of gentlemen opposed to the King, including the MPs for Shropshire, Bishops Castle and Shrewsbury. While these groups became official units of local government, their main function was to raise money for the Parliamentary army. Shropshire was expected to raise £375 a week, but, because so much of the county was in Royalist hands at the start of hostilities, the raising of this sum remained largely a dream.

The Castle's Fall to Parliament

It was the gentlemen of the Shropshire Committee who made the momentous decision on behalf of Parliament to fortify the small Shropshire town of Wem. From this garrison, assisted by others, a force set out under the leadership of Colonel Thomas Mytton to attack the town of Shrewsbury. At 4 a.m. on 22 March 1645, months after the King had left, Shrewsbury Castle fell to the Parliamentary side. A

Silver coinage, intended for army pay and much of it minted from plate given by local gentry. However, their offerings would not pass muster with the hard-headed soldiery, who refused this coinage on the grounds of the poor quality of the silver! Purer metal was requisitioned from Welsh silver mines.

small group had approached by boat along the river, crept in through St Mary's Watergate and managed to open the main Castle gate, to admit cavalry and infantry led by Colonels Mytton and Reinking. Both these officers later claimed the main credit for this coup! Fortunately, resistance was minimal and most of the garrison was allowed to leave. The Irish soldiers among them, however, hated because of atrocities committed by their compatriots earlier in the war, were mercilessly slaughtered.

The Ottley family of Pitchford Hall, painted by Petrus Troeuil. Sir Francis was one of several successive Royalist Governors of Shrewsbury.

For several gruelling months Shrewsbury acted as a garrison town, and its residents were to celebrate this fact for many years. On Cromwell's orders the town's defences were repaired and a new wall was constructed from the Castle, along the line of the river, to the Welsh Bridge.

By August 1645 the King's fortunes were on the wane and it was reported that he 'hath no more garrisons than only Ludlow, Bridgnorth and High Ercall' in Shropshire. By March, High Ercall and Bridgnorth (now home to Sir Francis Ottley, a former Governor of Shrewsbury, and his wife) had fallen to Parliamentary forces. Only Ludlow remained, and it too capitulated in May 1646. The fall of the King's headquarters of Oxford in June sealed the fate of the Royalist cause, although smaller-scale struggles continued until, and beyond, the ex-

Castle Gates House, where the first Earl of Bradford installed his mistress, Anne Harrison, in 1702. Intriguingly, he had this house, which formerly occupied the site of his own new house, taken down and rebuilt here.

The Newport Family

Sir Francis Newport came into possession of the Eyton Estate, near Shrewsbury, through his wife, who had inherited it from her father. His family retained close links with Shrewsbury for almost 200 years. In 1583 his nephew Edward, later to become the poet and diplomat Lord Herbert of Chirbury, was born here. Thirteen years later Sir Francis employed the Shrewsbury master mason Walter Hancock to help him develop the house and garden, building two 'banqueting houses' at each end of a bowling green (one of which is now available as a holiday let through the Vivat Trust, which has restored it.)

During the Civil War the Newports were fervent supporters of the King and, like others of their class, were penalised when Oliver Cromwell took power in 1648. However, at the Restoration of Charles II, Francis Newport was made Comptroller and Treasurer of the Royal Household and presented with the Castle, now without further military use. Newport later supported the accession of William and Mary and was made First Earl of Bradford.

The third Earl, in spite of a series of sexual misdemeanours, became Lord Lieutenant of Shropshire and was the most powerful political figure in the county at the beginning of the eighteenth century. His townhouse in Shrewsbury was used by the local council for many years and now awaits development as apartments.

ecution of the King on 30 January 1649. The princes Maurice and Rupert, who had both led armies for their uncle, were allowed to leave the country. For the next thirteen years the English Republic, led by Oliver Cromwell, was in control.

ELEGANT SHREWSBURY

'As in St James's Park . . .'
– Celia Fiennes, diarist and traveller

AFTER the Restoration of Charles II (1630–1685) in 1662, a more settled and relaxed society was able to develop in the midlands, as elsewhere. King Charles' lively court provided a thrilling model of urban sophistication which was imitated in provincial towns. In this region, leisure pursuits such as the theatre and horse-racing focused on Shrewsbury, which was beginning to acquire status as a successful and fashionable urban centre.

Shrewsbury's businesses continued to prosper and their proprietors to develop social polish, along with considerable self-confidence. The nickname of 'proud Salopians' may have been coined at this

The Bradford townhouse, built in tune with new standards of social elegance. For many years used by Shrewsbury and Atcham Borough Council as their offices and known as The Guildhall, the house will revert to residential use.

This fascinating view shows the fashionably laid out formal garden of a house in Dogpole at the end of the seventeenth century.

time after the burgesses' refusal of an offer by Charles II to make the borough a city. Ironically, in recent years the Borough Council has made unsuccessful attempts to attain city status.

Tea and coffee were recent, luxury imports and became the focus of much socialising – for men at least. A visitor, one John Mackay, at the beginning of the eighteenth century found 'the most coffee-houses that ever I saw in any town'. Among the town's 7,500 or so inhabitants were providers of a range of luxury consumer goods and services such as dancing lessons. There were fifty tailors, twelve barbers and nine tobacconists, as well as milliners, a furrier and a parfumier. Local gentry came to vote and discuss family and business affairs with

The new English Bridge by J. M. W. Turner, built in 1768–69 to the designs of John Gwynn. Many people in the late eighteenth century were eager to travel and visit attractive historic towns as well as 'picturesque' countryside. This early Turner drawing shows that, in an age before photography, views of Shrewsbury were saleable items for topographical artists to produce.

their lawyers. Their wives could make purchases and maintain useful social contacts. In 1725 when Daniel Defoe visited it, the town was 'pleasant . . . and rich . . . full of gentry and yet full of trade too'.

Before the Industrial Revolution gave a boost to road-building and other modes of transport, it was not easy to make short visits of any distance. Hence many landowners from outlying parts of Shropshire maintained a base in town from which to pursue their business interests and, increasingly, the gatherings that became a feature of upper-class life during the social 'season'. This idea of a fashionable time of year, during which the aristocracy and gentry would leave their country estates and assemble in resort towns for business and social activities, developed during the Restoration period. In Shrewsbury it was a time of further expansion: one of the areas of Shrewsbury developed for smart new housing was Abbey Foregate, on land made available by clearances for the new London to Holyhead road.

Celia Fiennes (1662–1741)

Celia Fiennes was an early example of the adventurous Englishwoman. Robust and intrepid, she travelled the length and breadth of the country, riding side-saddle and often accompanied only by her maid. Fortunately for later generations, she put her acute and intelligent observations down in a diary, although this was not published until 1888. This document, by an upper-class woman with access to the homes of many provincial grandees, offers a unique insight into the development of society at the end of the seventeenth century.

Not deterred by an unpleasant incident on her journey to Shrewsbury, when she was rudely jostled near Whitchurch by men she thought might be highwaymen, Celia Fiennes approved of the town. In particular she was impressed by the gardens laid out alongside the river by Shrewsbury Abbey. She commented that 'every Wednesday . . . most of the town, the Ladys [sic] and the Gentlemen, walk there as in St James's Park . . .'

Shrewsbury was one of the earliest towns in England to enjoy the benefits of a newspaper, first published in 1705 and confidently entitled *A Collection of all the Material News*. A more important publication, the still-flourishing *Shrewsbury Chronicle*, began life in 1772 and has been published weekly since before the American War of Independence. It was followed twenty-two years later by the *Salopian Journal*, and these two papers maintained opposing political views.

The Free Grammar School continued to offer education for boys, but as early as the 1690s there was also a school for young ladies, run by a widow, Mrs Esther Chambre. This establishment provided music tuition and deportment, and by the 1770s girls could learn French as well as dancing, music, writing and drawing at a number of schools.

Admiral Benbow

John Benbow (1653–1702) was a swashbuckling figure somewhat at odds with Shrewsbury's urbane social scene at this time. A sailor and commander of reckless bravery, he gained fame through his exploits at sea, among them the fierce defence of merchant ships against Moorish pirates. In 1698 he was a captain with the Royal Navy patrolling the West Indies, and he later became Commander-in-Chief of the King's ships. He died in a sea battle with the French.

Robert Clive (1725–1774), known as Clive of India.

The Corporation ran the town's financial affairs, maintained such public services as there were and dealt with issues of law and order. It ran its own Quarter Sessions four times a year as a forum for administration and the enactment of justice, and the town also hosted the county's Quarter Sessions. Visiting county gentry might take part in a Grand Jury together with members of the clergy and magistrates trying those charged with offences. An Assize Judge visited the town regularly to deal with serious crimes.

Elections aroused much popular interest and brought crowds of countryfolk into the town, although the franchise was limited to male householders and the lack of a secret ballot meant that the candidates could often browbeat their dependants into voting for them. Rival candidates would frequently vie with one another in entertaining potential supporters to food and drink.

One of Shrewsbury's leading political figures was Robert Clive. As Britain's influence overseas expanded, so did the role of those destined to create the new Empire, and Clive was one of these. He was born at the family home of Styche, near Market Drayton, in 1725, and his volatile personality made him something of a tearaway as a boy. His relatives were probably relieved when he joined the East India Company in 1742 and went to Madras as a member of its administrative staff in the military wing. The aims of the East India Company were at first purely mercantile, but military objectives accompanied the fierce commercial rivalry with the French, who were also busy trading with India. Clive rapidly demonstrated remarkable military ability, and, defeating the French decisively at the Battle of Plassey, he became Governor of Bengal. Effectively, he handed India over to British rule. Having returned as a hero with the usual financial rewards, in 1761 he became one of Shrewsbury's MPs, and was Mayor for the next year. The following year he purchased, first, the Walcot estate near Bishop's Castle, and in 1771 Oakly Park, probably with the intention of securing a political future for himself. Although his family remained hugely influential in the county, election to Parliament was never achieved without great expense of time and money in persuading shrewd local voters.

It is now thought that Clive suffered from manic depression, and, tragically, he killed himself at the age of forty-eight.

Leisure Pursuits

In Paris and London great parks became fashionable as settings for spectacular public entertainment, including music and fireworks. In 1719 Shrewsbury followed this trend, developing the Quarry Park to provide an elegant, outdoor, public amenity where ladies and gentle-

Avenues of trees were laid out in the Quarry, a sight admired by Dr Samuel Johnson, compiler of the famous Dictionary, *when he visited the town in 1774 in the company of his friend, the architect John Gwynn.*

This splendid grandstand was built by the Carline brothers, stonemasons and builders, for the Victorian racecourse at Monkmoor.

men could ride or stroll, meeting each other and showing off their expensive clothes and horses. Like Regent's Park, the Quarry was soon fronted by gracious residences.

Horses have always been a preoccupation of the English upper classes, and from 1718 one of the county town's social attractions was horseracing, held at Kingsland and Monkmoor and later at Bicton Heath, where the name Racecourse Lane survives. Race meetings were extremely smart occasions, and prizes were given by local gentry, including Lord Clive.

Shrewsbury's Enlightenment

A notable pupil of Shrewsbury School was the musicologist Dr Charles Burney, born in Shrewsbury in 1726 and later the father of the more widely known novelist Fanny Burney. Nevertheless, by the end of the eighteenth century, the School's reputation had moved into a spiral of decline. It suffered badly from poor standards, increasing curricular irrelevance and a damaging series of internal feuds. The second half of the eighteenth century was a period of intellectual ferment in Europe and one that saw the advancement of new educational theories. The town Corporation boldly undertook a major overhaul, appointing the great Dr Samuel Butler to bring the School up to date in tune with these ideals of the Enlightenment.

Dr Samuel Butler (1774–1839) was headmaster of Shrewsbury School for thirty-eight years, during which time the School's reputation was transformed. He raised the number of pupils from twenty to nearly three hundred by 1832. A powerful educational reformer, he is regarded as one of the founders of the English public-school tradition and was part of a group of enlightened people in the early nineteenth century living in and around Shrewsbury.

Some of these advanced thinkers were associated with the Industrial Revolution, for example Thomas Telford and the designer of the

Number 6 Quarry Place, designed by Thomas Farnolls Pritchard, Shrewsbury's leading architect. Houses such as this were often built speculatively by local builders hoping to cash in on the town's booming social status.

Ditherington Flax Mill, Charles Bage. Bage was an extraordinary figure: he was the town's mayor and among the founders of the Lancasterian School, but he was also a prolific designer and inventor who pioneered the idea of cast-iron building construction.

Many had developed philanthropic interests. The anti-slavery campaigner Archdeacon Joseph Plymley, with the help of his diarist sister Katherine, entertained members of this social and intellectual élite at their home, Longnor Hall. Like other educated men of his time, Plymley also concerned himself with turnpike roads and with improvements in farming, publishing *A General View of the Agriculture of Shropshire* in 1802.

Shropshire, with its richly varied terrain and extraordinary geological structure, was at the forefront of interest in geology. This was one of the passionate interests of the Plymleys' scientific coterie, and their contribution to the study of geology is of national importance

historically. Dr R. W. Darwin, the father of the great evolutionist, established a medical practice in Shrewsbury in 1786 and was a member of the group. As a child, Charles Darwin would certainly have been aware of these early scientific studies.

The statue of Charles Darwin, (1809–1882) outside his old school, which now houses the main public library. Darwin was born at the family home, The Mount, just over the Welsh Bridge. He was the official naturalist for the expedition of HMS Beagle *to South America, discovering and describing many new species of plant and animal. In 1859 he published his great work* On the Origin of Species by means of Natural Selection.

The Shropshire and North Wales Antiquarian Society had its own bookplate to adorn volumes in its substantial library. Most of its members were scholarly gentlemen of independent means and many were clergymen.

Along with the development of science and technology, the eighteenth century saw the rise of a new interest in the historic past. Antiquarian societies explored the remains of ancient British culture and amassed collections of artefacts. Nonetheless, with its focus on geological studies, Shrewsbury was relatively late in establishing its own antiquarian society. The Shropshire and North Wales Natural History and Antiquarian Society was founded in 1835 and it collected a range of organic and mineral materials as well as man-made items such as coins. These were laid out in a public museum and formed the basis of the modern Shrewsbury Museums' collections.

An example of the new breed of gentlemen-antiquaries was the Reverend Hugh Owen, whose book *Some Account of the Ancient and Present State of Shrewsbury* was published in 1808. In 1825 he and J. B. Blakeway produced a two-volume *History of Shrewsbury*.

The Castle: A Picturesque Monument

In the 1790s the new antiquarian interest made castles a source of romantic fascination, and the possession of one was something of a status symbol. Shrewsbury Castle was the property of Sir William

Owen and Blakeway's text was beautifully illustrated, as this engraving of a coin of Henry I (1100–1135), minted in Shrewsbury, shows.

Pulteney, the son-in-law of the Earl of Bath and said to be the wealthiest commoner in England. Pulteney wanted to create a suitably prestigious residence from the battered sandstone building on its rocky eminence.

For this purpose, he took the momentous step of introducing to Shrewsbury a talented fellow-Scot, Thomas Telford. Later to become far better known for his engineering achievements, Telford began his career as an architect. As well as converting the Castle Great Hall into a home, Telford designed Laura's Tower, an elegant and romantic

retreat for Pulteney's daughter Henrietta Laura (later Countess of Bath). This charming garden building on the remains of the old castle motte has a rococo interior deeply evocative of the late eighteenth century.

It was not uncommon for great landowners to fund locally raised regiments of militia, and the

Members of a re-enactment society, the Loyal Newport Volunteers. The original volunteers formed a local defence team at the end of the eighteenth century and are not to be confused with the militias, which were raised compulsorily.

Pulteney family were, partly for political reasons, ardent supporters of the Shropshire Militia. William, Viscount Pulteney, son of the Earl of Bath, founded the second of the two original regiments of what was later to become the King's Shropshire Light Infantry, on the basis that the officers would always support the family politically. Ironically, the viscount met his death on military service with the regiment in Spain in 1763. These Shropshire militia were particularly active during the Napoleonic Wars, when for a time a French invasion was feared. The first regiment was founded in 1755 or 1756 by another local grandee, William Whitmore of Apley, and the two amalgamated in 1881.

The Castle remained in private ownership until 1926, when the wealthy Shropshire Horticultural Society purchased it for the Borough.

In 1984 the Shropshire Regimental Museum was given a splendid new home in the Castle but, sadly, became the victim of terrorism eight years later when an IRA bomb caused fire damage to the internal fabric. The Museum reopened, with new displays, in 1994. Its attractive grounds are used regularly for events such as open-air theatre productions and concerts.

Public Entertainment

During the eighteenth century the town had several assembly rooms, as well as concerts and a new theatre, graced by the admired tragic actress Sarah Siddons and

The interior of the Shropshire Regimental Museum.

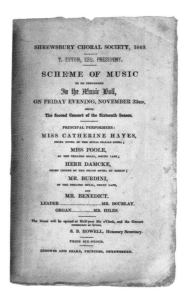

The programme for the first performance at the Music Hall in 1840. Before this time, concerts and balls had been held in the elegant assembly room at the Lion Hotel.

other stars of the day. One of these, born in Shrewsbury, was an extraordinary child actor, Master Betty. This boy became something of a craze in London and it was said that Cabinet meetings were rescheduled to allow ministers to attend his performances!

By the end of the eighteenth century the social season in Shrewsbury was extremely busy and there was an obvious need for a larger place of assembly, as well as for plays and concerts, than the Lion Hotel could provide. In 1832 Edward Haycock (who was also responsible for the Salop Infir-

The Recruiting Officer

The fashionable Irish playwright George Farquhar (1678–1707) was a soldier before turning to the stage as both an actor and playwright. During the War of the Spanish Succession he was sent to Shrewsbury to recruit men for the army and is believed to have stayed at the Raven Hotel in Castle Street (now demolished.) He clearly thought Shrewsbury well enough known as a 'smart town' to be the setting for his entertaining play *The Recruiting Officer*, which was inspired by his own experiences. The play, written in 1704 and dedicated to 'all friends round the Wrekin', features several lively characters based on real people of the town and its neighbourhood. All Farquhar's work shows evidence of an intelligent and good-humoured personality.

The Judge's Lodgings, accommodation for the visiting Assize Judge. Farquhar might have had a similar house in mind for the home of his Justice in his play The Recruiting Officer.

mary) designed the Music Hall in a prominent location on The Square. Twenty years later the venue hosted a play called *Mr Nightingale's Diary*, presented and performed by the novelists Wilkie Collins and Charles Dickens. Dickens returned more than once to give his famous readings there.

The popularity of a more proletarian event, held on Kingsland and later known as the Old Shrewsbury Show, was greatly enhanced by the arrival of the railway, which in 1852 brought 32,000 visitors. However, the Show was considered by respectable folk to be morally dubious, centring as it did on raucous 'entertainment' at the various arbours (see page 71) and on the Beehive public house close by. The Show was largely shunned by the middle class during Queen Victoria's reign and gradually became more and more sleazy. Shrewsbury School was desperately in need of new premises and these were available in the

The Music Hall, built in 1839.

Part of the great procession of guilds for the Old Shrewsbury Show, each one led by a mythological burlesque figure, such as the blacksmith god Vulcan for the smiths. This intriguing scroll-like drawing was the work of 11-year-old Samuel Hulbert and is nine feet long.

old building that had once housed the Foundling Hospital at Kingsland. The move was made following the Show's final abolition in 1882.

By the end of the nineteenth century the Old Show had been succeeded by two more morally acceptable celebrations, both economically important to the town in the twenty-first century. These are the agricultural show, held in early summer, and the now world-famous Flower Show.

8 — COMMUNICATIONS

L IKE other towns developed in the Saxon period, including Bristol, Stafford, Oxford and Worcester, Shrewsbury's promontory site was surrounded by marshland. This was, clearly, very convenient for defence, but the proximity of the river, with its potential as a route for transport and communication, was an important reason for the settlement's success.

In the tenth century the town was a strategic unit in the defence of the midlands against the Danes, a role maintained throughout the

The Old Welsh Bridge, by Paul Sandby. The bridge fulfilled an economic function for the town, enabling visitors to be taxed, especially those who had business to transact or livestock to sell in its markets.

medieval period when the military threat came from Wales. Later, as a county town, it benefited from the proximity of the principality as a market for Welsh goods and livestock, forming an important bridge-head for Welsh traders into the midland network of roads and water-ways.

Bridges

Whilst rivers were often used for defensive purposes, they also functioned as trade routes before the development of a road network. Market towns grew up along their banks from earliest times. Bridges were essential to the movement of merchandise, and Shrewsbury's bridges have a long pedigree. We know that there were two here in 1121. The Welsh Bridge was first referred to, as St George's Bridge, in a document of 1262. Like other such bridges, it had two towers, for defence

The new English Bridge, showing the dolphin carving. This watercolour by the nineteenth-century artist F. W. Seville, emphasises the solid dignity of John Gwynn's bridge design in contrast to its medieval predecessor.

A portrait of John Gwynn RA.

and for collecting the tolls that brought an income from outside traders. The final surviving tower was not taken down until 1770.

The eighteenth century saw increasing travel, both for commercial and leisure pursuits throughout the country. Both of Shrewsbury's main bridges were replaced with elegant robust structures quite different from their medieval predecessors. A bridge had existed on the 'English' side of the isthmus since the earliest days of the Abbey. By the 1760s the Old Stone Bridge, as the existing structure was then called, was clearly inadequate. The first stone of the new English Bridge was laid in 1767 to a design by the architect John Gwynn.

It was not until more than a century had passed that Victorian suburban development south of the river loop made a third vehicular bridge necessary. The cast-iron Kingsland Bridge was erected in 1872, followed by the pedestrian Greyfriars in 1880. A second pedestrian crossing came in 1923 with the elegant suspension bridge at Porthill, now such an attractive access point to the Quarry Park. This structure is now protected by Listed status. Today the river is crossed by several footbridges.

Turnpikes and Coaches
There was a coach service of some sort to take passengers to the capital from as early as 1681, when the coach from London travelled

via Newport Pagnell and Wellington. Regular coach services to London were available from the 1750s, running from public houses which could offer stabling and employ ostlers to care for the multitude of horses the operation required.

The Lion Hotel

John Ashby, the Town Clerk of Shrewsbury, was a shrewd entrepreneurial lawyer, tellingly described as 'guardian of many secrets'. To take advantage of the lucrative coach trade and at the same time satisfy the need for a fashionable place of assembly, he built the Lion Hotel next door to his own home. The Ballroom at the rear of the building has an elegant gallery and is decorated with delightful plasterwork tracery in the style of Adam.

However, it was the landlord of The Raven, Robert Lawrence, who in 1773 substantially furthered the interests of coaching when he introduced a new coach called the London and Shrewsbury Machine. This vehicle ran three times weekly from the Lion Hotel and managed to reduce the journey time to London to two days. Laurence's enterprise secured the Holyhead service and the lucrative Irish mail trade for Shrewsbury.

In 1780 he became landlord of the Lion, and it was this hotel that thereafter became most closely associated with Shrewsbury coaching. During the reign of Queen Victoria the novelist Charles Dickens was a guest at the hotel on no fewer than three occasions.

A naïve painting of a coach at The Lion Hotel. Some of the coach names expressed their characteristics, such as 'The Stag'", 'Dart', 'Rocket' and 'The Bang-up', the last sounding somewhat alarming for older passengers!

The age of the stagecoach was ushered in by vastly improved roads, as a result of the introduction of the turnpike system. Hitherto local people had been expected to maintain their roads, leading to an enormous variation in standards across the country. The exaction of tolls to be paid at the turnpike gates transferred these costs to road users. In 1725–26 the first Shropshire road came under this system, and within fifty years well-maintained turnpikes had immeasurably improved communications, allowing horses to travel at much greater speed on the smoother surfaces. This revolutionary change led to the development of the stage coach and the faster, more efficient delivery of mail. The post-coach business required large numbers of horses, running in teams of four which were changed every seven to ten miles. These animals were looked after carefully in order to maintain their fitness and worked for no more than one hour in every twenty-four. As a result, the post-coaches were immensely successful, covering, among other routes, journeys to Birmingham, Chester, Hereford and Aberystwyth. In 1785 the London to Bath mail coach was travelling at twelve miles an hour and other journeys achieved speeds of up to sixteen miles

Samuel Hayward and 'The Wonder'

The eccentric coachman Samuel Hayward became a well-known character. He was renowned for driving his team of four smartly -groomed horses at extraordinary speed, including a final spectacular gallop up the Wyle Cop and into the yard of the Lion Hotel. Driving Shrewsbury's most famous coach, 'The Wonder', in 1825, he left at 5 a.m. by St Julian's clock and arrived in London sixteen hours later. The journey required 150 horses, and the changeovers, at coaching inns along the route, were effected in five seconds. In 1838 another record was set when 'The Wonder' left London at the same time as the Euston train and arrived twenty minutes earlier! Hayward was also known for his grumpiness and long silences, maintaining that one could not talk and drive. He died in 1851 and his plain gravestone can be seen in St Julian's churchyard.

By the middle of the century the heyday of coaching was over and 'The Wonder' sadly came down in the world, ending its days as a mere two-horse vehicle between Shrewsbury and Birmingham.

an hour. In 1807 the Shrewsbury Post Office started a service across the Welsh mountains to Aberystwyth. This left the Lion and Unicorn inn at 4 a.m. and arrived the same evening.

By the early 1830s, the high point of coaching, a journey to London, which had once taken several days, could be covered in thirty-six hours. Other inns offered coaching services and, because of their convenience, continued to run well after the coming of railways.

Many of the improvements to the road network can be attributed to the great engineer Thomas Telford. Between 1815 and 1836 he developed the A5, a spectacular fast, new road to Holyhead. Described by historian Barrie Trinder as 'the best road in Europe', it ran from London to the ferry crossing to Ireland and was partly financed by the government. Telford hoped that this road might pass from Wellington to Chirk, avoiding Shrewsbury, but this was impossible and much unfortunate demolition occurred, in particular that of the Abbey cloister.

Waterways

It was, however, the River Severn, navigable as far as Welshpool, that continued to provide the town with its main trade artery. This had been the case since the Middle Ages and, until the creation

Two steam trains cross the viaduct into Shrewsbury in 1849.

A Severn trow at Frankwell Quay. These barge-like boats were a standard form of freight transport, pulled by men along the towpaths. They were large cargo vessels of between forty and eighty tons with a main- and topmast eighty feet high carrying square sails. Frequently they carried a second mast.

early in the nineteenth century of a towpath for horses, the barges were pulled by brawny young men. Naturally this group, known as 'bow-hauliers', acquired a fearsome reputation for drunkenness and general wildness.

Mardol Quay was constructed in 1607 to facilitate the loading and unloading of goods at this important spot in the town, where the tanneries and other industries were located. The owner was required by the authorities to operate a tariff discriminating heavily in favour of locals, permitting 'all manner of barges of all persons to unload at the said quay, taking for every barge-load of wood or coal 12d . . . for a ton of other goods – off a burgess 2d and off a foreigner 4d.' A year later it was found necessary to construct a second quay, on the Frankwell side of the river. By this time barges were supplying the town with luxury goods such as coffee, tea, wine, tobacco and spices. By the 1750s a weekly wherry was taking passengers to Gloucester, and in 1756 there were 376 trows operating from Shrewsbury.

The enhanced importance of waterways following the Industrial Revolution, spearheaded in Shropshire, led to the development of canals. The Shrewsbury Canal, intended to bring coal to the town and link up with the network that connected to the River Severn at Ironbridge, was opened in 1793. This led to extraordinary feats of engineering: at Longdon, for example, the canal passed over the River Tern on one of the first iron aqueducts, and at Berwick the canal featured a tunnel that was nearly 1,000 feet long. The canal was linked with the early railway under the banner of the Shropshire Union Company, but the freight train quickly became paramount and the use of waterways dwindled, although the canal basin at Castlefields, which formed the terminus of the Shrewsbury Canal, was not finally abandoned until 1922.

The Railway

As early as the seventeenth century, cast-iron rail tracks with trailers pulled by horses had been pioneered in the east Shropshire coalfield and the Ironbridge Gorge. However, the steam train as a freight and passenger vehicle did not come to Shrewsbury until 1848. Unfortunately, those with long-distance business to attend to had begun to shift their patronage elsewhere.

However, this economic slide was reversed later in the century when Shrewsbury became the focus for express trains from one end of the country to the other, servicing the new seaside and country holiday traffic as well as commerce. This brought such an increase in traffic to Shrewsbury that in 1899 an extraordinary engineering venture provided the Gothic-style station with a third floor, dug under the existing structure. During the 1980s the station was recognised for its architectural quality and refurbished.

Although the main line to London was electrified in 1967 as far as Wolverhampton, Shrewsbury's importance in the railway network then changed as it ceased to be a main line destination.

In the 1980s Shrewsbury was linked to the country's motorway network by the M54 and a northern bypass followed, opening more

The Railway Station as it was built in 1848, to a design by Penson of Oswestry.

areas north of the town for the development of the twentieth century's out-of-town retail and business parks.

Communications within the county and the sense of community solidarity have been enhanced and developed by BBC's introduction of Radio Shropshire in 1985.

NINETEENTH-CENTURY INDUSTRY AND SOCIAL CHANGE

A S QUEEN Victoria's reign moved forward with its enthusiasm for spas and the seaside, Shrewsbury ceased to be seen as a smart resort town. This was partly a result of the growth of democracy. The introduction of the secret ballot in 1872 finally ended the corrupt system whereby the local gentry controlled voting and had themselves and their sons elected to Parliament. This had often been achieved by bribing potential voters with copious amounts of alcohol! Hence their presence among the electorate, supported by their town houses, was no longer profitable and they retreated to their country estates, preferring to travel by train to spend the social season in London. The railway, boosted by the success of the Great Exhibition in 1851, enabled greater numbers of ordinary people to move round the country.

Following a period of agricultural decline at the end of the nineteenth century, the beginning of the new century was again a period of expansion. The town was an important

Pride Hill in 1854.

The Square, by C. W. Radclyffe, showing its appearance at the time of Disraeli's election. To the left can be seen the old Shire Hall, demolished in the 1970s.

focus for the railway network connecting its rural hinterland and much of Wales with the midlands and London. It boasted a prestigious railway station and a large railway hotel opposite. It was also a garrison town for the King's Shropshire Light Infantry, a busy livestock market and an administrative and social centre.

Benjamin Disraeli

In 1841 Shrewsbury played a part on the national stage when the somewhat controversial young Benjamin Disraeli (1804–1881) was elected to Parliament as a Member for the town. Later to be twice Prime Minister and a major founder of the British Empire, Disraeli was also an influential novelist. In his youth he travelled widely and acquired a reputation for eccentricity. Notoriously bad with money, he accumulated large debts and some hostility. During his campaign in Shrewsbury, angry opponents chased and tried to ambush him. Fortunately the young politician had married a wealthy woman with considerable social skills of her own, and she lost no time in entertaining voters lavishly in various hostelries. Her husband addressed the public from the balcony of the Lion Hotel.

The maltings' interior, with hops drying.

New industry was developed as a result of more modern technological advances. While the production of flax in Shropshire had not been a commercial success, brewing continued to be a major industry in the town. The pioneering building at Ditherington became a maltings in 1898.

Birds of Passage

Following the arrival of the railway, Shrewsbury, like other market towns, attracted a wide range of visitors and accommodated them in a variety of more or less reputable inns. One in Hills Lane, opposite what is now the Museum, had a stunning range of guests in 1861. Three were itinerant traders, two were carpet weavers, while others were a livestock drover from Somerset, a Welsh tailor, and a plate engraver, perhaps present to make views of the old town as tourist souvenirs. The most exotic guest was Asam Ali, a 44-year-old vendor of tracts, born in the Islamic holy city of Mecca and married to an Irishwoman!

In the same year, further down Hills Lane, there were two travelling musicians from Sardinia, while the Castle and Falcon played host to Charles Durlane, a 'professor of ventriloquism'!

Education, too, was becoming a priority, provided at first by voluntary religious bodies (mostly Church of England) advised by the government. The school buildings usually consisted of one large room or hall where children of all ages were taught, with one or two smaller rooms for older pupils. There was a charitable school as early as 1708 in Shrewsbury, and another was provided for in the will of draper Alderman Thomas Bowdler, in 1724, 'for the instruction, clothing and apprenticing of poor children of the parish'. A further philanthropic venture was Allatt's School, founded in 1798 with a magnificent bequest from the former Chamberlain of the Corporation, John Allatt. The two elegant houses, one each for schoolmaster and mistress, were designed by Haycock with a linking arcade and can still be seen on Town Walls.

The population of Shrewsbury increased by 45 per cent between 1801 and 1871, when it reached over 23,000, largely a result of the increase in prosperity brought about by the railway. The mostly Vic-

Brewing was a major industry in the town and this large factory at the bottom of Bridge Street housed the Circus Brewery.

Coleham Pumping Station, restored by the Shrewsbury Steam Trust. In its heyday the large beam engines required teams of seven men to keep them running, consuming a ton of coal every day! With their handsome brass and copper fittings they formed something of a municipal showpiece.

torian suburb of Castlefields grew up around the canal basin close to the commercial centre of the Butter Market and the Benyon Street flax mill. The expansion of business connected with the railway gave the suburb added importance for speculative builders.

By the middle of the nineteenth century many of Britain's urban communities had been hit by serious epidemics of cholera, and, as a consequence, sanitation and public health had become more widely discussed. Shrewsbury's sanitary facilities were inadequate to the needs of the greatly increased population and there were outbreaks of cholera here in 1832 and 1849, during which as many as two hundred and fifty people died. This crisis occurred in so many towns nationally that the government responded in 1848 with the Public Health Act. Shrewsbury introduced street-cleansing services and other efforts, but these did little to improve the quality of local water. Public health problems became worse.

The natural flow of the River Severn is broad and shallow, and evil-smelling, polluted mud flats extended across its course close to residential areas. It was obvious that something had to be done, and so in 1894 the Borough Council undertook a massive sewer replacement scheme, accompanied by the construction of a steam-operated pumphouse at Coleham. Raw sewage was pumped from the new station under the river and away from the town to a treatment works at Monkmoor by means of two large steam-operated wheels.

Shrewsbury continued to develop as a major market town and in the Victorian period boasted a Corn Exchange and Market that brought ecclesiastical grandeur to the retail trade. Sadly, it was demolished in the 1960s to facilitate the building of the present market hall.

The Lancasterian School at Castlefields taught boys and girls according to the system devised by reformer Joseph Lancaster, who visited the town in 1811. By 1891 between forty and fifty older children were being taught according to a relatively advanced curriculum that included science, art, mathematics and French. In 1926 the School was transferred to the local authority.

Morris & Company

Morris's, founded in 1869, is a family business that since its inception has contributed to the life of the town and exemplifies aspects of social change here. The founder, James Morris, started out in a candle-making factory in Frankwell and became a very successful general grocer. His four sons, led by the eldest, J. K. Morris, continued the business, dealing in lubricating oils and moving into other areas such as bakery and catering. The splendid Pride Hill department store contained a café which could seat three hundred people – and a ballroom!

The charismatic head of the firm until 1935 was known simply as 'J. K.' An energetic reformer and philanthropist, he was elected as this conservative town's first Labour councillor. The Morris Hall, Bellstone, was built at his expense for the local Labour Party's use.

Soon the company was running a string of grocers' shops which became small supermarkets.

Morris's continues to thrive and provide considerable local employment. The firm has bought land judiciously and now, in tune with the increasing tendency in commerce towards service provision, is engaged in the expanding market of nursing and residential care.

(Opposite) Severe flooding. (Above) Withers' Borough Carriage Works were coachbuilders for horse-drawn and motor vehicles in the early years of the twentieth century. The works occupied a site by the river, close to the present-day Shrewsbury Hotel.

In 1912 the building of the weir at Castlefields became necessary for reasons of public health, low water in summer being a potential source of disease. The weir deepened the water and facilitated some boating and angling. However, because the river is so shallow it is still prone to severe flooding. This perennial problem, affecting the flood-plain throughout the length of the river Severn, has been exacerbated by climatic change and other environmental factors, for which a satisfactory solution has yet to be found.

In 1900 the first commercial garage in Shrewsbury was opened, and sixteen years later the first motor bus arrived. Until the end of the 1970s the bus station was immediately in front of what is now Shrewsbury Museum and Art Gallery.

10 THE BUILDINGS OF SHREWSBURY

'Buildings gay and gallant, finely wrought . . .'
—Thomas Churchyard, 1587

SHREWSBURY'S street scene is immensely attractive and adorned with many buildings of great interest. All that this volume can attempt is a very truncated overview, omitting much. There are, however, other publications on this subject readily available. Visitors entering Shrewsbury through Frankwell, or from the English Bridge up Wyle Cop, receive an impression of black-and-white timber-framed buildings, and this is not misleading. A large proportion of the fabric of the town dates from the mid-fourteenth to the late sixteenth century, a time of general prosperity here. It should be pointed out, however, that this appearance is a feature of Victorian conservation measures, relying on bitumen, and then of visual taste. When originally built, most of these structures would not have had their timbers picked out in this way.

The earliest buildings we know of in Shrewsbury are those revealed by archaeology. Traces of possible Saxon buildings have been located near Pride Hill, and in this area, along the line of the old town walls, excavation in the 1970s revealed the remains of substantial early medieval stone halls. These were the homes of wealthy merchants, and, as some

View of Mardol by Thomas Shotter Boys. This charming view of c.1830 demonstrates the high quality of the Shrewsbury street scene in the early years of the nineteenth century. It is remarkable that in Shrewsbury the old street pattern, established before the end of the twelfth century, has survived intact. The illustration on the opposite page depicts Butcher Row; the arch leading to Pride Hill no longer exists.

of their garden plots have been shown to lie beyond the line of the walls, they must have been laid out before the walls were built in the 1220s. The surviving buildings are probably rather later in date. The interior of more than one can be seen today in shops on Pride Hill, as a result of archaeological work in 1959–60. In particular, Bennett's Hall of c. 1250 (in 2004 The Bank retail store) has an elaborate fireplace and doorways.

As a building material, stone possesses obvious merits against the very real danger of fire, but its use at this time is a particular status symbol associated with wealthy individuals. Some went even further in their desire to impress: Sir John de Charlton, an important royal

Vaughan's Mansion, drawn in 1780, was probably erected in the fourteenth century around an earlier core featuring an upstairs hall. Remodelled many times over the years, this hall is now incorporated in the Music Hall.

administrator (see page 47), was 'licensed to crenellate' or create an impressive battlement effect on the roof of his home in 1325. This status symbol was a relic of more warlike times when only the King's military henchmen were allowed fortified residences.

Very little survives of the timber-framed structures of the fourteenth century although at the fascinating King's Head public house in Mardol dendrochronology has revealed a hall of 1403–04 within a structure largely a century younger. Following a serious fire on Wyle Cop in 1426, Nicholas Clement, a brewer, bought a large plot of land, probably for speculative purposes. Here he erected a box-framed industrial unit at Barracks Passage, and, the following year, Henry Tudor House, fronting Wyle Cop (see page 38). All these buildings have been attractively restored by the conservation architects Arrol and Snell.

The Abbot's House, owned by Lilleshall Abbey, of 1456, is an example of the later medieval phase of building, and although it may have been used by the Abbot as a town residence it is more probably what would now be called an investment property, yielding rental income. The ground floor was given over to shops. Unusually, the existing frontage, with shutters which would have opened downwards to form trestles, is of original date. A similar frontage can be seen in the courtyard of the Old Post Office, Milk Street.

The Great Build

Although the countryside of Shropshire can boast a series of imposing stone houses, Whitehall, at the end of Abbey Foregate, is the only great stone house in the town. Like Condover Hall and the Abbey, it is built of soft, Severn Valley red sandstone. Erected between 1578 and 1583 by a successful lawyer, Richard Prince, it demonstrates an

An engraving depicting Whitehall.

almost square 'double pile' design. Like Madeley Court and Upton Cressett hall elsewhere in the county, it has its own gatehouse. The roofscape, so often a feature of Tudor buildings, is elegantly completed by a glazed cupola. This attractive structure is a 'banqueting room' to which guests would adjourn for the consumption of dessert and to admire the view while the great hall was cleared of its trestle tables in preparation for entertainment. Used for many years by the Department of Health and Social Security, Whitehall awaits redevelopment as apartments. The square plan was known in Europe but appears for the first time in England in this house. Because of this, and the convenience of its service rooms housed in the basement, Whitehall represents a huge advance in domestic amenity and is a landmark in building history.

The second great period of construction in Shrewsbury, towards the end of the sixteenth century, coincides with a spate of building across the whole country, initiated by prosperous farmers and merchants rather than great aristocrats. Shrewsbury shared in the building boom which resulted from the prosperity brought by the wool trade and developed its own highly individual carpentry designs, seen to impressive effect in the nearby country house Pitchford Hall. This spectacular black-and-white house has boldly projecting wings and gables patterned with elaborate quatrefoil carpentry, a style of decoration now identified with Shrewsbury.

In spite of the fact that stone was the chosen material for houses of the country gentry and wealthy farmers, timber was preferred in towns. This was not only because the layout of long, thin burgage plots allowed only a small area of house to face the street but also because wood was cheaper than stone or brick. A far more decorative effect on a small surface space, indicating the owner's wealth and status, could be achieved with timber patterning, and it was visually effective at close quarters within the street. By the end of the sixteenth century oak had acquired a cachet because it was in short supply and therefore more expensive, so it was possible for the better-off merchant to impress aspiring rivals.

Almost opposite Owen's Mansion stands the handsome but much less decorative Ireland's Mansion, erected as a speculative tenement venture. Many such buildings offered shops at ground level with living accommodation above, declining in facilities and respectability the higher one went. The topmost attics were reserved for the poorest residents.

Many timber frontages represent medieval houses up-

The process of re-fronting an older house can be seen here, where an eighteenth-century front is superimposed on a timber building.

graded by the owners during the latter half of the sixteenth century, a process which was to occur again in the Georgian period.

Civic Pride

'Magnificent municipal structures that no neighbouring town could equal.'
— Eric Mercer, architectural historian

The absence of grand private residences at the end of the sixteenth century is evidence of the shift to a new sense of civic independence and dignity in the town. This is reflected in public buildings such as the Market Hall of 1596–98 and the rebuilding of Shrewsbury's Free Grammar School. Both are constructed of stone from Grinshill, to the north of the town, and the Market Hall is believed to be the work of the master mason Walter Hancock. Hancock was one of very few masons at this time who had the skill to draw plans, which, in his case, incorporated new features derived from the Italian Renaissance. (He is probably the architect of the magnificent Condover Hall.)

The Rowley's House and Mansion complex, now Shrewsbury Museum and Art Gallery, demonstrates the move from timber-framing, in the warehouse building, to brick for the adjoining residence. William Rowley was a Shropshire brewer who became a Shrewsbury burgess in 1594 and decided to settle in the town. Among his commercial premises was a timber-framed warehouse, to which in 1616 he added a mansion for himself and his family. This fine brick house has a faintly Dutch air appropriate to the private residence of a leading merchant who had achieved the status of gentleman. Origi-

Remaining as a fine landmark for the east side of town, the younger Haycock's massive Doric column commemorates Lord Hill, whose family seat was at Hawkstone north of the town. 'Daddy Hill', as the popular general was known to his troops, was the Duke of Wellington's right-hand man in the Peninsular War.

nally its gardens extended almost to the banks of the river, where there were commercial wharves.

Later, between 1694 and 1700, the first Lord Bradford built him-self a townhouse which, with its hipped roof and pedimented dormer windows, combines Renaissance ideas of classical elegance and tradi-tional English simplicity in what has come to be called the Queen Anne style. This house functioned for many years as the headquar-ters of Shrewsbury's Borough Council and was known as the Guildhall(see illustration on page 86).

Millington's Hospital, Frankwell, with its pedimented pavilions and central block, is unique in the county in demonstrating the influence of the Italian classical architect Palladio. It was built by Edward Massey and Richard Scoltock. Little more is known of these two Shropshire builders than that Scoltock built a chapel for Shrewsbury's small Roman Catholic community in 1776. Sadly, no trace of it remains.

T. F. Pritchard (1723–1777)

The most notable of Shrewsbury's architect-builders is Thomas Farnolls Pritchard. The son of a joiner, he benefited from the increase in prosperity and consequent rapid expansion of better-quality housing during his lifetime. At his workshop on Pride Hill he assembled a team of excellent craftsmen, in particular the plasterer Joseph Bromfield, whose work may be seen in certain private homes in the town. Pritchard began to acquire a higher social status and in about 1770 moved out of town to live like a country gentleman at the remains of the old Newport family home, which he rebuilt, at Eyton-on-Severn. Thereafter, his work focused more on bridges, and it is believed that he designed the first cast-iron example at Ironbridge. By the time of his death the profession of architect had become properly recognised.

Although Pritchard was employed widely across the midlands and Welsh march, much of his work can still be seen in Shrewsbury, in particular Swan Hill Court and the church of St Julian.

The first decade of the seventeenth century was an architectural watershed. Shrewsbury was being transformed from a town of 'good houses, mostly old buildings, timber', as described by the travel diarist Celia Fiennes in 1698, into a residential environment of smart streetscapes. Some of these Georgian dwellings were actually from an earlier period, re-faced in tune with the change in fashion. Abbey Foregate was developed as a smart suburb, as was the area round St Chad's church, Belmont and St John's Hill. Between Celia Fiennes' visit and the middle of the eighteenth century the character of the Swan Hill area changed radically. Previously inhabited by poor textile workers, it became an 'upmarket' neighbourhood for county families visiting the town for the social season.

The tradition of public philanthropy continued to appeal to these people, and in 1747 Millington may have hoped to impress his contemporaries with a startlingly modern design for an almshouse (offering accommodation for poor elderly people).

An interesting Scottish architect achieved two great works in the county of Shropshire. In the early 1790s George Steuart, the designer of Attingham Hall at nearby Atcham, saw his innovative plan for a new St Chad's church completed. The very fine rotunda is based on the classical idea of a circular temple and is linked with an elliptical anteroom and octagonal tower. The new church was made necessary by the sudden collapse (foreseen by Telford) of the ancient red sand-stone church, of which only the Lady Chapel still stands.

Nearby and slightly later is a handsome early nineteenth-century terrace by local men, Carline and Tilley. They belonged to a group of architect-builders of modest scope but considerable competence in adapting fashionable urban styles to the needs of their clients.

By the end of the eighteenth century the profession of architect was universally acknowledged and Shrewsbury had produced a crop of successful builders whose designs were admired and who, unlike the smart London architects a day's coach journey away, could supervise construction in person. Pritchard led this group, which included Bromfield, Carline and John Hiram Haycock.

Close to the Buttermarket stands the magnificently rusticated entrance to the prison, designed by John Hiram Haycock (1759–1830) and built by Telford. It features a bust of the prison reformer John Howard.

Swan Hill Court, built for the Marquess of Bath in 1761 by Thomas Farnolls Pritchard. With its somewhat squashed-looking flanking pavilions, this is a town mansion using the grand model more usual for a country residence.

It was Hayock's son Edward (1790–1870) who was to benefit from a new shift in European taste in the early nineteenth century. Following his success in the competition to design a monument to Lord Hill at the end of the Napoleonic Wars, the young architect was able to take advantage of the enthusiasm for a revival of Greek styles. These harked back to the earliest and purest 'primitive' Greek temple-building. Although the Greek Revival was somewhat slow to make an impact in provincial Shropshire, Haycock deployed aspects of the style effectively before 1815 in his design for Allatt's School, and later for the Salop Infirmary and the Music Hall.

The Buttermarket, Howard Street, was also built in Greek Revival style. Standing with masculine dignity at the terminus of the Shrewsbury Canal, it foreshadows many other great commercial structures of the transport industry. Its immense interior is supported on cast-iron columns.

Much of Shrewsbury's nineteenth-century development was sub-urban, across the river from the congested older centre. During the 1830s the Cherry Orchard area close to the Abbey was developed with pleasant middle-class terrace houses. Later, on the elevated Kingsland site close to Shrewsbury School's new premises, large brick mansions with spacious gardens were built for the most prosperous. Following the cholera epidemic of 1849 the need for improved housing for the working class became more pressing. Ground behind the prison in the Castlefields area was developed by a Freehold Land Society, part of a movement aimed at giving shareholders building plots. Today this terraced housing has become attractive to young professional people seeking homes close to the town centre.

Twentieth-Century Building

Since the beginning of the twentieth century Shrewsbury has been a conservative town not noted for architectural innovation. However,

The Priory Boys' School, now the Sixth Form College, designed in a 1920s Queen Anne style by the versatile Frank Hearn Shayler (1869–1954). This intriguing architect was a friend of Lutyens, with whom he cycled round France and Holland in the 1880s. His own house on The Mount (called The Red House after William Morris' of that name) skilfully employs the Arts and Crafts style. During the 1930s Shayler turned his hand to the modern International Style, designing 21 Ridgebourne Road and 31 Shelton Road.

St David's Presbyterian Church of Wales (1935–36) was designed by the West Bromwich architect Cecil Fillmore. The brick building uses Tudor motifs but is entirely modern without being obtrusive.

there are one or two exceptions. In the town centre, the Alliance and Leicester building at the corner of Shoplatch and the High Street demonstrates an air of flamboyance and almost of art nouveau. It was designed by a Shrewsbury man, Lloyd Oswell, who was also responsible for the red-brick Halifax Building Society premises, a lively addition to the streetscape of the High Street with its seventeenth-century-style Dutch gable. Close by, the National Westminster Bank of 1926 is a good example of neo-Georgian.

A more recent commission for Baart Harries Newall was the graceful showroom for Mansers Antiques. This adroitly planned building occupies an important site by the English Bridge, at the entrance to the historic core of the town. It combines a glazed, forty-five-degree corner with a river-fronting façade in perfect sympathy with the adjacent Victorian townhouses.

Unfortunately, much of immense historic and architectural interest in Shrewsbury was destroyed during the 1960s, and what has replaced it is often of poor quality. The Market, with its overbearing clock tower, does little to enhance the street scene although the Lloyds/TSB Bank building of 1970 at the head of Roushill perhaps surprisingly maintains visual links with older styles. The widespread destruction of this era has caused local people to become even more fiercely protective of the remains from the past, and there is little of architectural interest dating from the second half of the twentieth century.

In the 1980s and 1990s Shrewsbury sought to re-invent itself as a shopping centre and the old Infirmary building was elegantly converted by the conservation architects Arrol and Snell to form apartments and a small-scale shopping mall.

Some corporate patrons have demonstrated more boldness with buildings that make signature contributions to the townscape. An interesting response to the challenge of a very restricted sloping site is the County Council's Shropshire Archives building of 1995, with its storage below the pleasant public area. Integral to the design are at-

Shropshire Archives.

tractive exterior features, including planting around the forecourt and an external staircase rising steeply from the bus station.

An example of more consciously modern design is the Learning Centre of Shrewsbury Sixth Form College by Baart Harris Newall, completed in 1996.

MODERN SHREWSBURY

THE OPENING of the twentieth century saw Shropshire once again involved with advances in technology. During the First World War the Royal Flying Corps was keen to demonstrate the new opportunities offered by air power and members demonstrated these by flying Sopwith Camels from an airfield at Tern Hill. The RFC, a forerunner of the Royal Air Force, also established a large depot at Harlescott. The county's regular infantry regiment, the King's Shropshire Light Infantry, based at Copthorne Barracks from 1881 until 1968, has throughout its history served with distinction across the world. In the First World War no fewer than four thousand of its men were killed.

Harlescott's role as a location for industry was reinforced when in 1915 the Sentinel Waggon Works was set up there. Sentinel

Away from its twentieth-century industries, Shrewsbury remained the visual magnet it had always been for artists. P. W. Owen ARPS, a remarkable photographer, here captures the romance retained at the town's urban heart.

soon became internationally renowned as a producer of steam-powered lorries and high-pressure chain-drive equipment. The firm had originated in Glasgow in 1875 and, following the success of steam engines, began experimenting to create a haulage vehicle that was itself powered by steam. Through family connections with the Horsehay Ironworks east of Shrewsbury, the Harlescott site was selected as being suitable to provide access to the midlands conurbations as well as to the ports of Liverpool and Manchester.

Here, in July 1915, No 1102, the first waggon to bear the Shropshire registration letters 'AW', proudly took to the road. During the First World War all production went to the armed forces and indeed many civilian steam waggons were commandeered for military use. The first machine was partly superseded in 1923 by the 'Super Sentinel', which was exported to Kenya, South Africa, the Middle East and what are now Zambia and Zimbabwe. In the same year the first steam locomotive appeared; it was later described in the *Sentinel Transport News*:

'This little locomotive proved itself such a glutton for work and so extraordinarily economical that the experienced railwaymen who saw its performance were incredulous that it could do all that it did do, and use such little fuel in the process. . . . Within just fifteen months of the first they (Sentinel) had completed and standardised three types of locos, the largest of which is capable of handling heavy goods trains or fast suburban passenger traffic.'

By 1930 the firm was producing engines for aircraft and buses and, between 1954 and 1958, tractors, but in 1956 it had been taken over by

The Sentinel trademark. The existing works building still bears the model sentry over its entrance.

Rowley's House and Mansion (now Shrewsbury Museum and Art Gallery) from Hills Lane in 1908, by Evacustes Phipson.

Rolls-Royce Motors Ltd and shortly afterwards converted entirely to the production of diesel engines. Most Shropshire people, however, remember the firm as Perkins Diesels Ltd, a Peterborough company that took over the site in 1985 and a couple of years later were providing work for more than twenty-eight thousand employees. The site is now in the hands of Caterpillar, who are operating an environmentally friendly machine recycling business, but staff numbers are reduced to about two hundred.

The Sentinel company was also responsible for the garden suburb in this area, known then as Sentinel Village. Laid out in 1919 in tune with new utopian theories of town planning, it offered spacious and pleasant housing for the workforce as well as playing fields and informal recreational space. Each house had six rooms including, unusually for the time, a bathroom, and was heated by electricity supplied from the works powerhouse.

Shrewsbury's Writers

Housman's famous lyrical verse sequence *A Shropshire Lad* was written prophetically just before the First World War. At the time he wrote it, the poet had a knowledge of the countryside that was somewhat sketchy, but a writer whose work is very firmly located in the Shropshire landscape is Mary Webb (1881–1927). She lived for a time in Bayston Hill and in her popular novels wrote lovingly of the countryside she knew so well. Her best-known works are *Precious Bane* and *Gone to Earth*, the latter being made into a film.

The great war poet Wilfred Owen (1892–1918) lived with his family in Monkmoor Road before his enlistment and tragic death in the trenches of World War I. His monument is in the grounds of the Abbey. As a boy he had written lyrical verse of a somewhat derivative nature, but his experience of the horrors of the battlefields of Flanders forged a completely new and extremely powerful voice. 'The poetry', he wrote, 'is in the Pity.' He remains probably Britain's best-known war poet.

More recently, the 'Brother Cadfael' novels of Ellis Peters were set in twelfth-century Shrewsbury.

Partly because of the employment available here, much of Shrewsbury's earlier twentieth-century development was concentrated in Harlescott. The livestock market, which continued to flourish, outgrew its location on Smithfield Road and moved here in the late 1950s. At the end of the twentieth century further development has taken place to the north of Harlescott, offering commercial and retail space, and the livestock market is expected to move again, to benefit from improved accessibility in this area offered by the extended road network.

This character of the area remains decidedly commercial. The emphasis of suburban development shifted to the south of the town during the 1930s when a new bypass (now the inner ring road) brought more development to Meole Brace, Bayston Hill and elsewhere. At this period areas of slumlike congestion in the centre of the town were demolished, much of it very ancient timber-framed structures that today would be protected. However, discoveries were also made and the late Tudor complex now known as Rowley's House was revealed close to Barker Street.

Wartime Shrewsbury

Shrewsbury's experience of the Second World War was largely free from the bombing suffered by more important urban centres, apart from an incendiary bomb and two high explosive devices that killed three people in a cottage on the Ellesmere road. Five bombs were dropped at Shawbury in June 1940, but it was the requirement of a universal night-time black-out that actually caused more casualties.

However, as in the rest of Britain, Shrewsbury's resources were entirely absorbed in the war effort. In 1939 the Ditherington Flax Mill became a barracks for training army recruits and the town was filled with thousands of servicemen from training units there and at Shelton. There were military bases at Shawbury and Donnington and of course the existing King's Shropshire Light Infantry barracks at Copthorne. First-aid posts were everywhere, and people rapidly became familiar with sandbags and the sounds of sirens. Women in uniform, including the ATS, were a surprising vision, and female telephone engineers even more so. Shropshire's traditional rural hinterland has always focused on the county town, and cattle continued to be driven through the streets to the market on what is still called

Evacuees

As a country town some distance from the main industrial targets of Hitler's bombs, Shrewsbury became the destination for many thousands of people evacuated from Merseyside and the West Midlands conurbation. These evacuees, lodging with frequently reluctant local families, were mothers with small children, but the largest group consisted of unaccompanied schoolchildren. They came from a number of different schools and shared a double-shift system in Shrewsbury with the two Priory schools. Evelyn Robinson, billeted rather grandly with the Mayoress and her daughter, recalls how, following lessons in the morning, she and her friends, all twelve-year-olds, would run riot through Woolworths and other shops in the afternoon! One of the boys, Kenneth Taylor, later wrote poignantly of his delight in the change: 'I did not know there could be such lovely scenery. I did not know there could be so much sky. I'm sure there was not nearly so much, and it was usually grey, at Liverpool.' Another evacuee was so homesick that he stole a bicycle and pedalled back to Birkenhead.

Smithfield Road. Because the farms were now deprived of men, the Women's Land Army in their khaki cord jodhpurs soon became a familiar sight. Moreover, everyone was gardening: as part of the 'Dig for Victory!' campaign to encourage self-sufficiency in food, even the Quarry Park was used for growing crops.

For eighteen months from the summer of 1940, Shropshire played host to a foreigner of high status in the European scene. Charles de Gaulle, the charismatic leader of the Free French, lived temporarily at Ellesmere, where he and his wife rented Gadlas Hall. The strong-minded General's tall figure was a familiar sight to passengers at the Station travelling to and from London.

Everybody of working age was in uniform, unless they were mothers of young children, and older men were actively involved in Civil Defence. Shrewsbury firemen and police distinguished themselves in offering assistance to bomb-devastated Coventry after the raid in 1940.

In 1942 the American GIs arrived. Although often described as 'oversexed, overpaid and over here', generally they were welcomed. They often behaved with generosity, throwing a large party for Shrewsbury children at the Granada cinema. The Raven Hotel became an American services club. and in October of that year the town was treated to a baseball match between the Flying Eagles and the Yankee All Stars. This featured a host of colourful characters with names such as Dead Eye Delaney, Walloping Wood, Slinking Hank and Snooty Shneider. Jessie, the company donkey, was evidently still on the staff of the Ditherington Flax Mill in 1944 and was mobilised to give rides to Meole Brace children at a VE-Day party!

The first post-war agricultural event, the West Midlands Agricultural Show, was held in 1946 and the large numbers attending astonished the organisers. The Agriculture Act of the following year gave further impetus to farming in the county, although its traditional industries were in decline. Shrewsbury has since time immemorial been the focus of a widely distributed farming economy and the town con-

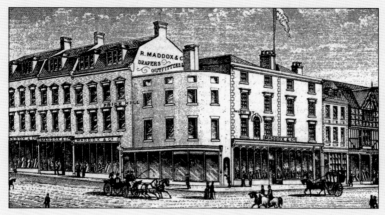

Maddox & Co.

Maddox's, the smart Shrewsbury department store, was initially advertised as the 'Shropshire Carpet, Drapery and Outfitting Warehouse', offering '"plain and fancy furnishing, mantle and dress-making' as well as, rather oddly, 'funerals'. Always to the fore with popular schemes, the company made a huge contribution to the patriotic effort in many different ways during the Second World War, even maintaining a large allotment garden to grow vegetables. It also endowed a cottage home for a blind person and never lost an opportunity for propaganda, which must have benefited its sales even more than the war effort!

tinues to host the Show, which attracts visitors from a wide area from Wales and across the midlands. The two-day event had to be suspended during the disastrous foot- and-mouth epidemic of 2001, and two years later it was moved from its traditional slot in May to a date in June. It now features a large range of recreational displays and attractions for non-agricultural visitors. Like the Flower Show, it is a source of pride and affection for local people, and there are anxious hopes that it will continue to thrive and survive the grave crises besetting British farming in the early years of the twenty-first century.

The Shropshire Horticultural Society, founded in 1885, has moved from strength to strength and its Flower Show during August has been an event of international repute for over a hundred years. It was further promoted during the 1960s by the presence of the celebrated gardener Percy Thrower, then employed by the Borough Council. In 2003 the Flower Show, held in the Quarry Park, attracted eighty thousand visitors.

Serious efforts were made to maintain sport in the town during the war years and Shrewsbury benefited from the presence of charismatic players such as Billy Wright of Wolverhampton Wanderers. In April 1941 four thousand people watched the Shropshire Cup Final between the RAF and Wellington. Following the war, Shrewsbury Town Football Club was elected to the Football League.

Since the end of the war the fortunes of Shrewsbury have improved, although during the 1960s, a time of expansion in British higher education, the town failed to grasp the opportunity, with all the associated cultural and economic benefits, of hosting a new university.

Culture, Heritage and Tourism

During the twentieth century the town's cultural life continued to be served by the Music Hall with a programme of plays and concerts. The Shrewsbury Orchestral Society, under its dedicated conductor F. C. Morris was able to attract soloists of the renown of Myra Hess, Eileen Joyce and Louis Kentner.

Although the town's horizons have inevitably remained somewhat provincial, Shrewsbury Borough Council maintains an excellent museum and art gallery displaying objects associated with the town's past as well as material excavated at Wroxeter. It reflects Shropshire's status as a seedbed of geological enquiry and has a thriving programme of highly regarded art exhibitions.

Shropshire has a varied tradition of musical appreciation, and The Jazz and Roots Club, housed atmospherically at the Buttermarket, presents live bands from Africa and South America and attracts audiences from across the region. The county as a whole supports thriving and high-quality amateur drama groups, and the Old Market Hall

---

Shrewsbury School's Old Boys

Shrewsbury's famous School has launched a number of distinguished twentieth-century individuals, among them the novelist Neville Shute and, more recently, the Conservative politician Michael Heseltine, born in 1933. The broadcaster and music writer John Peel and the satirical journalist Richard Ingrams were members of the post-war intake, along with the comic talents Willie Rushton and Michael Palin. The artist Sir Kyffin Williams attended the School before the last war, as did a series of distinguished lawyers, including Geoffrey Lane, the Lord Chief Justice from 1980-92. Sir Colin McColl was Head of MI6 from 1988 to 1994. Sir Neville Cardus (1889–1975), the author and cricket writer, was on the staff.

---

is now a successful cinemaand digital arts centre and runs a lively late-night café. In spite of the restrictions of its nineteenth- century building, the Music Hall continues to present a varied programme, and the town authorities are planning a new theatre building.

Shrewsbury has been a beneficiary of the popular interest in heritage that has developed since the 1960s. This, combined with its location near to the Ironbridge Gorge and in beautiful countryside full of ancient monuments, has made the town a centre for tourism. The Roman city of Wroxeter, a source of fascination and investigation for nearly two centuries, is only five miles away. During the years before and after the First World War, this extensive site – which, unlike other Roman cities, has never been built over – was excavated more thoroughly than ever before with extremely rich results. Among those early diggers was the late, great Sir Mortimer Wheeler.

Archaeological surveys and some excavation have been a feature of the town centre's experience in the last quarter of the twentieth century. During the 1960s the expansion of the shopping area, coupled with legislation which made it incumbent upon urban developers to set aside time and money for excavation in appropriate areas, led to the examination of important sections of the old town wall, revealing parts of several medieval merchant halls (large homes). Later, as part of a development along Old Potts Way, excavations revealed details of the Abbey Mill and guest accommodation, including a kitchen. The County Council has produced excellent popular books on the archaeology of Shrewsbury Abbey, which was brought to life in the 1980s and 1990s through the hugely popular fictional character Brother Cadfael. (Sadly, the location for the television version of these novels by Ellis Peters, set in the twelfth century, was not Shrewsbury.)

In the year 2000 Shrewsbury Borough Council adopted an archaeological strategy designed to maximise the benefits of the historic environment for the town and its people as well as to protect the resource for the future. There is avid interest in archaeology locally, and an annual forum at the Shire Hall publicises continuing fieldwork.

In 1968 the KSLI became part of the Light Infantry based in Winchester, but Shrewsbury retained its traditional links with the Army. The Copthorne barracks is now the Headquarters of the Fifth Division, and Shrewsbury Castle houses the Shropshire Regimental Museum.

In 2004 Shrewsbury and Atcham Borough Council moved to a more user-friendly building on Frankwell by the riverside.

Fireworks at the Shrewsbury Flower show, held in the Quarry Park.

'Pedestrianisation' of the town's main thoroughfare at the end of the 1970s, followed by improvements to traffic management and the general streetscape in the 1990s, have helped the development of attractive specialised shopping. At the end of the twentieth century the recolonisation of the town centre for residential use gained pace, and several old buildings have been converted to form smart flats for the growing number of childless professional people. The Tourist Information Centre organises daily guided tours of the town during the summer.

The 600th anniversary of the Battle of Shrewsbury in 2003 aroused considerable popular interest, and the town is making attempts to capitalise on its most celebrated son, Charles Darwin. The International Music Festival, which brings young people to the town from all over Europe, takes place in Shrewsbury every summer.

In 1974 local government was reorganised and the boundaries of the larger, modern Borough of Shrewsbury and Atcham were drawn. The population has since risen to nearly one hundred thousand. At the beginning of the twenty-first century further changes, towards a regionally based form of government, are being considered.

However, Shrewsbury's psychological allegiance is not attached to the conurbations of the west midlands but rather, as throughout its long history, to the rural counties of the Welsh border and their urban centres.

INDEX